Texas Tales
In Words and Music

Larry D. Hodge

Original Songs and Music
by Michael Stevens

Texas Tales
In Words and Music

Larry D. Hodge

Original Songs and Music
by Michael Stevens

Republic of Texas Press
Plano, Texas

Library of Congress Cataloging-in-Publication Data

Hodge, Larry D.
    Texas tales in words and music / text by Larry D. Hodge ; original songs and music
by Michael Stevens.
       p. cm.
    Includes bibliographical references and index.
    ISBN 1-55622-794-9 (pbk.)
    1. Texas—History—Anecdotes.   2. Frontier and pioneer life—Texas—Anecdotes.   3.
Texas—Songs and music.   4. Frontier and pioneer life—Texas—Songs and music.
    I. Stevens, Michael, 1945- II. Title.

    F386.6 .H63 2001
    976.4—dc21
                                          00-046470
                                              CIP

Republic of Texas Press is an imprint of Wordware Publishing, Inc.
No part of this book may be reproduced in any form or by
any means without permission in writing from
Wordware Publishing, Inc.

Printed in the United States of America

ISBN 1-55622-794-9
10 9 8 7 6 5 4 3 2 1
0009

All inquiries for volume purchases of this book should be addressed to Wordware Publishing, Inc., at 2320
Los Rios Boulevard, Plano, Texas 75074. Telephone inquiries may be made by calling:

(972) 423-0090

Dedication

For Lucy Mason Hodge,
who had ranch dust in her blood
and farm dirt under her fingernails.
She told many wonderful stories
but
furnished a poor example for a writer:
I never heard her tell a lie.

The authors owe many thanks to the following individuals:

To Reaves Nahwooks of Cache, Oklahoma, for providing the Comanche phrase "those who have gone on" at the end of the Cynthia Ann Parker piece, as well as his insights into the Comanche religion;
to Larry Seyer, "the ear" at Electric Larryland, without whose incredible talents this album would never have turned out so well;
Alice Stevens;
Nine Francois and Marielle Glasse;
and Ginnie Bivona at Republic of Texas Press.

Contents

Introduction

There's a powerful big difference between writing stuff you want to write and grinding out stuff for the money. The main feature of this difference is that you get paid for writing the latter, which makes your wife, your dog, your cat, your banker, and all the other folks you keep fed a lot happier.

But writing just for the money does precious little for your own soul.

Much of my writing—both the meat and the sweet—has been about Texas and Texas history. I've had a hand in writing and editing Texas history textbooks for the fourth and seventh grade levels in every state adoption since 1970. This experience has made me pretty particular about facts. I prefer to use ones that are true.

J. Frank Dobie, perhaps the greatest of Texas writers on Texas history and folklore, said in his preface to *The Longhorns* that he was "a teller of folk tales, and as a historian I have not hesitated to use scraps of folklore to enforce truth and reality." Dobie could get away with that, but I can't. However, I have borrowed freely—though selectively—from his work (and that of many others), for this book and its associated sound recording may not be held to the same strict standard of accuracy as textbooks are and should be. The opportunity to break loose a bit from the bonds imposed by textbook writing and its requirement to be politically correct, nonoffensive, noncontroversial, and often downright dull made this project a pleasure.

Researching stories for *Texas Highways* and *Texas Parks & Wildlife* magazines and several guidebooks has enabled me to travel throughout Texas, seeing places and meeting people it would never have been my privilege to know otherwise. Traveling Texas and writing about it have cemented a lifelong love affair with the state and afforded me the opportunity to live out every person's dream, to do what I love to do and get paid for it.

I have already admitted that I am not the writer J. Frank Dobie was, and I hasten to point out that I am not the singer Michael Stevens is, either. In fact, my singing talents are such that no living person, myself included, has ever heard me sing. I will not sing even in a sun-warmed shower laid atop a boulder in the remotest reaches of the Big Bend. I fear there would be global consequences in addition to a die-off of local flora and fauna.

Nevertheless, I serve a vital function in the musical world. Singers need listeners, and I am a listener of the finest quality. I don't cough, fidget, sing along, talk to my neighbor, or visit the concession stand or other facilities in the midst of a performance. I laugh in the right places, cry in the right places, stomp my feet only when asked to, and applaud as long as anybody else is clapping.

Michael and I set out to bring you a collaborative work that combines the heart and feeling of his music with a lively and accurate accounting of the historical background of each song. We hope it will bring you as much pleasure as it has brought us.

Larry D. Hodge
Texas Hill Country

❧ 1 ❧

The Old Chisholm Trail

ONE OF THE REASONS THE STORY of cowboys and trail drives has such widespread appeal is that it involves ordinary people doing extraordinary things. Those who rode the range and trailed herds up to Kansas and beyond knew they were expanding the bounds of human experience. That made them feel special, and that feeling was reflected in the songs they made up about themselves and their doings. These were proud people living a bold and adventurous life in dangerous times, and they tended not to be modest when rhyming out, however imperfectly, verses telling of their exploits.

Many people make the dual mistake of thinking all cowboys are singers and all singers of cowboy songs are cowboys. Most real cowboys couldn't carry a tune in a tow sack and had, as Ramon Adams said, a voice like a burro with a bad cold. The cowboy's instrument may not have been melodious, but it had been fortified by a career of yelling at cows and horses, and it was strong. They didn't sing good, but they sang loud. As one tale goes, a cowboy helping move camp was inspired to pour out his feelings in song, and the cook promptly stopped the chuck wagon and jumped down to grease a squawking axle.

Cowboys sang about the life they knew and the things that happened to them. Judging by the myriad verses in "The Old Chisholm Trail," most of the things that happened were bad, but the truth probably is that cowboys focused on the things that made their lives different and more exciting than the humdrum existence of a banker or store clerk. They liked to sing about the troubles they had; in a perverse form of one-upmanship, each tried to paint his troubles as worse than anybody else's.

Despite being unqualified to sing in public without risking humiliation or punishment, most cowboys felt no

Railhead towns such as Abilene and Wichita, Kansas (shown here), gained a well-deserved reputation as places where hard-living cowboys could be quickly separated from their pay.

The UT Institute of Texan Cultures at San Antonio, No. 73-1601

hesitation in composing verses to add to songs, and "The Old Chisholm Trail" became so long a cowboy could probably have sung a verse a mile from San Antonio to Dodge City and never repeated himself. Most of the choicest verses have been lost, for they were far too ripe to be put into print in those times.

The readiness with which cowboys could add to the song is illustrated by Ramon Adams' story about a South Texas cowboy out for a spree. He followed every drink with a rendition of another verse of "The Old Chisholm Trail." At last, fearing the cowboy's singing would sour the whisky, the bartender invited him to leave. The cowboy high-stepped his way onto the porch, which was five feet off the ground, and burst into another verse as he neared the steps:

With my knees in the saddle and my seat in the sky,

I'll quit punchin' cows in the sweet by and by,

at which point he managed to miss the steps completely and sailed to the ground below, landing standing up and still staggering. Missing nary a beat, he bellowed,

And, by God, they shore built them steps damned high.

Francis Abernethy cut pretty near the bone when he said of the song that it "is not a complaint or a moan or a blues. It was no list of grievances; it was a catalog of commonplaces, of experiences that were natural to their lives, and there was a certain amount of brag implied in the song. The cowboy lived a hard and sometimes dangerous life, and this gave him a difference that set him apart from the usual run of men. He was proud of the fact that he was a part of a group of men who could endure, and 'The Old Chisholm Trail' is his laugh at adversity."

The melody of "The Old Chisholm Trail" was borrowed, it is said, from a Stephen Foster tune called "Old Uncle Ned."

* * * * *

The Old Chisholm Trail

Trad.
arr. Stevens/Seyer

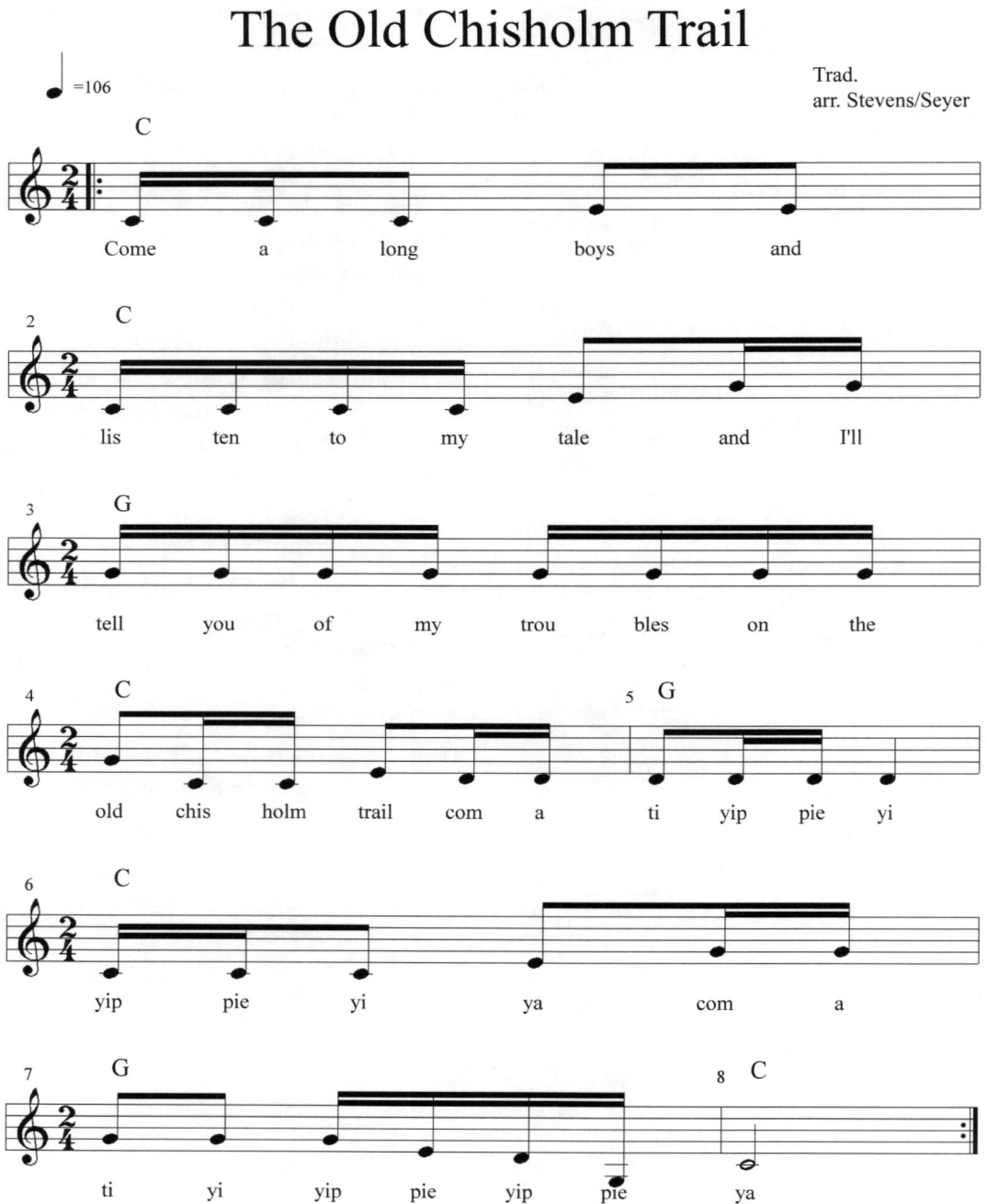

Come along boys and listen to my tale
I'll tell you of my troubles on the old Chisholm trail

(chorus)

Coma ti yippie yi yippie yi ya
Coma ti yi yippie yippie ya

I started up the trail October 23rd
I started up the trail with the 2-U herd

On a ten dollar hoss and a forty dollar saddle
I'm a gone to punchin them Texas cattle

I woke up one mornin' on the Chisholm trail
With a rope in my hand and a cow by the tail

My feet in the stirrups and seat in the saddle
I hung and rattled with them longhorn cattle

Stray in the herd and the boss said kill it
So I shot 'em in the rump with the handle of the skillet

Oh it's beans and bacon most every day
I'd as soon a be eatin that prairie hay

I'm on my best horse and I'm goin at a run
I'm the quickest shooting cowboy that ever pulled a gun

I went to the boss to draw my roll
He had me figured out nine dollars in the hole

I'm up in the mornin' afore daylight
And afore I sleep the moon shines bright

Come along boys and listen to my tale
I'll tell you of my troubles on the old Chisholm trail

Rare is the kid growing up in Texas who does not aspire at some point to be a cowboy, or at least the popular image of what a cowboy was. I had my chance at the age of six, when along with all the other kids in the first grade I was drafted to take part in the annual Christmas program at Elgin Elementary. My mother found the money somewhere to make the assigned cowboy outfit for me, complete with chaps made of a length of oilskin tablecloth material of suitable pattern.

I recall for certain only two things about my brief career as a cowboy. One is that the end of the program did not arrive in time for me to make it to the bathroom safely. The other is that the shirt my mother made for me out of feedsack material showed a cowboy in purple pants, green shirt, and red hat—pretty much the typical drugstore cowboy look —roping a yellow cow. I know this not because my memory is that good, but because scraps of that shirt later found their way into a quilt top my mother made, and that quilt hangs in my stairwell today.

My mother grew up on a ranch her father bossed in Bastrop County. She married a farmer, and when we kids were old enough to work in the fields beside her, the stories she told of the glamorous life of the cowboys she knew enabled her, like an agricultural Pied Piper, to make us kids hoe peanuts fast enough to keep in earshot and not miss any of the story. I was

grown before I realized what she'd been up to.

Late in her life she accompanied me and my wife, Sally, on a trip to South Texas, and on the way home I put in a tape of Arlo Guthrie songs. I don't think she much appreciated his song about motorcycles, and I'm pretty sure the lyrics describing smuggling drugs in from London went over her head. We were sailing along on Highway 16 somewhere below San Antonio, near the main stem of the Old Chisholm Trail, when suddenly I became aware of a voice from the back seat singing along with Arlo: "Way down yonder in the Indian Nation, a cowboy's life is my occupation, in the Oklahoma hills where I was born." That's the first I knew that my favorite song on the album was also hers. I'm sure she knew "The Old Chisholm Trail" as well and likely heard it sung by cowboys who had traveled that path.

A lot of cow boys and a few cow women went up the Old Chisholm Trail, and I have no doubt that my mother, had she been born in time, could have been one of them. Like them, she radiated quiet good humor, competence, and inner tranquillity. Like them, she was happy to be who she was, and to hell with what anybody else might think. She reminded me of something J. Frank Dobie had to say about one of the most famous cowboys of all, Charles Goodnight: "He himself had never been afflicted with the itch for being noticed—that pimply outbreak on small natures who cannot abide with equanimity their own smallness."

I'd like to think that something of that in her rubbed off on me as we traveled that branch of the Old Chisholm Trail between Birth and Death.

The Chisholm Trail

The roots of the Chisholm Trail, the longhorn and the ranching industry, reach far back into history. Ranching began on the Iberian Peninsula (in what is now Spain) sometime after the year 1000. Dr. Joe Graham, author of a book on South Texas ranching heritage, attributes the development of ranching in Spain to four factors. "There were men who understood cattle, large areas of unoccupied land too arid to farm but covered with grass, a breed of cattle good only for beef and hides, and the tools to work the cattle with."

When Columbus and later explorers came to the Americas, they brought the cattle, the men, and the knowledge of ranching with them. They found in Mexico and Texas the other essential ingredient: grass.

Most people assume that cattle ranching is about raising cows. It's not. Ranchers are grass farmers, and cattle are the combines they use to harvest their crop. Dick Kleberg of the King Ranch recognized this when he said of the ranch's huge Santa Gertrudis cattle, "Cattle are

machines to gather and sell grass. We want a big rack to hang the grass on."

The Spanish brought at least three breeds of cattle to the Americas. These animals interbred and, over centuries, evolved into a long-legged, narrow-bodied, hot-tempered, long-horned critter that could survive just about anywhere on its own. That's exactly what they had to do in Mexico and Texas, and they not only survived, they thrived.

The Spanish breeds blended with other breeds, and the result was the Texas longhorn. Running wild on the grassy prairies, they learned to fight off wolves, bears, and mountain lions and hide from people in river bottom thickets, emerging at night to graze. As spooky as deer and as vicious as wounded buffalo, they were little used for beef, generally being killed for their hides and tallow.

When the Civil War ended in 1865, some five million longhorns roamed loose in Texas. Barbed wire had not been invented; most of Texas was public land; railroads were almost nonexistent; money was scarce. Virtually the only resource the war-impoverished state had in abundance was cattle, but this was a mixed blessing. The longhorns were so wild that "to kill one you would have to stalk it as you would a deer," a cavalry officer wrote. Wounding one was not a good idea. A cow-hunter said, "If I had my choice, I should prefer a wounded bear to a wounded bull, half a dozen times over."

Even before the Civil War, Texas ranchers had driven cattle to out-of-state markets on a small scale. These drives had blazed trails to Missouri, Louisiana, and California, but they had also aroused the enmity of farmers along the way, for the Texas cattle trampled crops and carried ticks that infected the farmers' cattle with a fatal disease, Texas fever.

People were not unaware of other dangers attendant to this enterprise. In an 1860s precursor to the song "Mommas, Don't Let Your Babies Grow Up to be Cowboys," a Denton newspaper writer counseled, "Do not allow your boys to load themselves down with Mexican spurs, six-shooters, and pipes. Keep them off the prairies as professional cow hunters. There, in that occupation, who knows that they may forget that there is a distinction between 'mine' and 'thine'? Send them to school, teach them a trade, or keep them at home."

However, after they'd seen Appomattox, there was no keepin' 'em down on the ranch.

Now Texans had just one chance to rebuild fortunes smashed by the war, and they seized it wholesale. A cow brute worth $4 in Texas might bring as much as $40 in the North. The problem was getting the cow to the market. The cattle drive was the solution. That much they knew. What they needed was a trail to follow that would get them to market without encountering too much trouble with farmers.

Jesse Chisholm provided the answer, even though he died about the time cattle drives began to move over the path that would bear his name.

Chisholm was an Indian trader and guide. Born in Tennessee about 1805, he was half Scot and half Cherokee. Throughout his life his sympathies lay with the Indians. When the first Cherokee lands in the Southeast United States were taken from them and the Cherokees were forced to move west to Arkansas, Jesse Chisholm traveled that bitter path with them. For forty years he served as a guide and interpreter, trying to smooth relations between the whites and the Indians. He set up a number of trading posts in his travels. He also rescued a number of white captives from the Indians and returned them to their families. Both whites and Indians trusted Chisholm; the Indians called him "the man with a straight tongue."

During the Civil War, Chisholm lived at the present site of Wichita, Kansas. Near the end of the war, he and a partner loaded a train of wagons with goods and went south into the Indian Territory, where they set up a trading post at Council Grove on the North Canadian River, near the present site of Oklahoma City. Thereafter Chisholm regularly made trips between the two points, bringing cattle, buffalo robes, and furs north and sending trade goods south. Soon other traders followed his wagon tracks across the prairie.

Always a peacemaker, Chisholm persuaded the Plains Indians to attend the peace conference in 1867 that led to the signing of the Medicine Lodge Treaty. He died the next year, not knowing that soon millions of longhorn cattle would follow the trail he had blazed across the Indian Territory, nor that cattle drovers would give his name not just to the part of the route he laid out, but to the entire length of the trail from southern Texas to

Campsites on trail drives were chosen for convenience, not comfort. The chuck wagon was the closest thing to home cowhands had for months at a time. How many actually read books in camp is unknown.

The UT Institute of Texan Cultures at San Antonio, No. 73-58

Kansas. It was a fitting tribute to a great pioneer.

Two out of three parts necessary for the great drama to begin were now in place. Texas drovers were willing to risk their lives to drive their cattle to market. Jesse Chisholm had marked the trail for them to follow. All that was needed was someone to buy the cattle, take delivery of them, and arrange for them to be shipped north.

It was a daunting undertaking, but the perfect man for the job had already been in training for several years. Joseph G. McCoy, a young cattle dealer from Illinois, had begun thinking in 1867 about finding a way to set up a new market for Texas longhorns. The market would have to be on a railroad, and it would have to be far enough west to avoid problems with farmers.

McCoy took a trip on the new Union Pacific Railway as far as Salina, Kansas. The train was delayed a while at a bump on the prairie called Abilene, and McCoy scouted the area while he waited. Railroad officials were not optimistic about the prospects. When he talked to them about establishing a shipping point for Texas cattle somewhere in central Kansas, he got a drenching with cold water. "It looks too visionary, too chimerical, too speculative, and it would be altogether too good a thing to happen to us or to our road," one said. Another told him, "It occurs to me that you haven't any cattle to ship and never did have any; and, I,

sir, have no evidence that you ever will have any.... Therefore, you get out of this office, and let me not be troubled with any more of your style."

McCoy could not believe the shortsightedness of the railroad moguls, but he still firmly believed in his idea. He took the Union Pacific out to Solomon City, west of Abilene, and located an excellent site for his stockyard. However, local citizens pooh-poohed the idea, and McCoy returned in disgust to Abilene, then a frontier village with a dozen log homes, a few log business houses, and a hotel with a grand total of six rooms. McCoy bought 250 acres on the northeast side of the little burg and set about building his own sure-enough town, soon to be called Texas Abilene.

In two and a half months McCoy had built shipping pens that could hold a thousand cattle, installed scales, and erected a barn and an office. He had under construction a three-story hotel complete with billiard room, bar, and a dining hall that could seat 250; a livery stable; and a bank. He persuaded the railroad to put in a hundred-car siding, and he got the governor of Kansas to write a letter endorsing the project. In addition, McCoy had handbills sent to Texas towns telling of his work, and he hired a friend to ride out, meet with drovers who were holding cattle in the Indian Territory waiting for a buyer, and tell them McCoy was waiting in Abilene with cash. Soon clouds of dust to the south foretold the arrival of the first herds. At last, Texas drovers had the market they had been looking for.

It took time for the name Chisholm Trail to catch on, but within a few years it was firmly established. Like a giant Christmas tree, it sprawled from the Rio Grande to Abilene, side branches feeding in to join the main stem running from Brownsville to San Antonio, Austin, Waco, Fort Worth, and on to Red River Station, crossing the Indian Territory, and striking the Kansas border at Caldwell and thence on to Wichita, Newton, and Abilene. Later, as the Atchison, Topeka, and Santa Fe Railroad built westward from Kansas City, running well south of the Union Pacific tracks, a new market developed at Dodge City. This in turn led to a new trail, actually a westward extension of the Chisholm Trail, that left the original path at Belton in Central Texas and angled northwest through Fort Griffin, crossed the Red River at Doan's Store, and closely paralleled the eastern edge of the Texas Panhandle, grazing the northeast tip, until it struck almost due north to Dodge.

To borrow a phrase from modern-day military recruiters, driving cattle up the Chisholm Trail wasn't just a job, it was an adventure. It was also part of a way of life that set cowboys apart. They were different from others, what they thought of as lesser mortals, and they dressed and acted the part with unbridled enthusiasm.

People who didn't know better sometimes accused the cowboy of "puttin' on airs" about his clothing and gear, but the fact is that centuries of cow tending, beginning with the Spanish, led to the development of implements as necessary to the cowboy life as horses and wide open spaces. Nothing about the cowboy's gear was just for show: He carried everything he owned wherever he went and of necessity took along only what he had to have. Of course, being human and not a little proud of himself, when he could he flashed a little style, but every article about him was still functional.

The cowboy's chaps, derived from the Spanish *chappareras,* were indispensable leg armor when chasing longhorns out of the thorny South Texas brush. His "war bonnet," or hat, had a wide brim to shade eyes and neck from the blazing sun or, on many occasions, the pouring rain. It also did good service as a water bucket, bellows for starting fires, and signaling device. The cowboy could throw it into a charging cow's face to confuse her long enough for him to mount a horse or a fence, and in cold weather he could take his bandanna and cinch the brim around his ears to keep them from freezing.

If the cowboy had a theme song, it would be the clump of high-heeled boots pounding out a rhythm to the jingle-jangle of his spurs. The cowboy usually spent more for a pair of boots than he did for a horse. As much as working atop a horse, wearing boots and spurs set the cowboy apart. The boots' high tops helped protect the lower legs from brush, rocks, and the chafing of stirrup leathers. The high heels kept the cowboy's feet from sliding through the stirrups, and when he was roping from the ground, the high heels dug in for traction. The underslope on the heel made it less likely to hang up in the stirrup if the cowboy was thrown. The pointed toes guided the foot into the off stirrup when mounting a horse.

Spurs had a variety of names, from grapplin' irons to persuaders to can openers to hell rousers. As vicious as their sharp-pointed rowels looked, however, spurs were not for the purpose of "gigging" a horse. Spurs were used as a reminder, not as punishment. A cowboy who cut a horse was soon looking for another job. When quick action was needed, all the cowboy had to do was press the sides of the rowels into the horse's flanks and hang on.

Other personal gear the cowboy toted included the slicker, or "fish"; the bandanna, or "wipes"; and the bedroll, or "velvet couch." The main purpose of the slicker is made clear in these lines from "The Old Chisholm Trail":

It's cloudy in the west and a-lookin' like rain,

My dern ol' slicker's in the wagon again.

However, the slicker served a variety of purposes. It made a saddle cover when it rained and a saddled horse had to be left outside. When training horses, the cowboy rubbed his slicker over it to get it used to being touched everywhere. Life being what it is, though, as the song relates, the slicker was often somewhere else when it was needed for its intended purpose.

A cowboy's "wipes" was one of the smallest things he owned, but it was one of the most useful. It helped shade his neck or, pulled over the face, kept dust out of his mouth and nose. It could tie down a tall hat in a high wind or keep a norther from blowing his ears off. It strained water drunk from muddy waterholes and, rinsed out after being used as a washcloth, muddied clean ones. It mopped sweat from his brow and made a pretty fair holder for a hot branding iron. It could blindfold a skittish horse or hobble one at night. Bandannas made slings for broken arms, tourniquets for arms and legs, and bandages for wounds. More than one badman was "handcuffed" with a bandanna, and in a few cases the strip of cloth substituted for a hang rope. When the cowboy's whole world went to hell in a hand basket with him close behind, his bandanna kept the dirt out of his face as he rested a while in a lonely grave on the prairie before heading off to that great roundup in the sky.

Western movies and TV shows would have you believe the west was won by hardy souls who carried only a canteen and a pair of saddlebags—always

Real cowboys bore faint resemblance to the version popularized by dime novels and, later, movies and television. These two South Texas cowhands probably wore their best clothes to have their picture made but lack sartorial splendor nonetheless. It's doubtful both were southpaws; more likely this was a daguerreotype, in which the image was reversed.

The UT Institute of Texan Cultures at San Antonio, No. 68-282

conveniently empty to receive any gold they found. These celluloid cowboys sleep in the open with their saddle for a pillow and their hat for a blanket. The man who had to sleep on the ground every night wanted and needed all the comfort he could get and still carry with him.

Cowboys didn't own much, but what was theirs they kept in their bedrolls and "war sacks." Inside a waterproof tarpaulin, made so the cowboy could snap himself up inside, he kept a couple of heavy quilts, or soogans, and maybe a blanket. Sometimes there was a feather pillow. On rainy nights there was room to stash his hat, rope, boots, and spurs inside. Cowboys who thought a lot of their horses took their bridles to bed with them, too, on cold nights, so as not to put cold steel into the horse's mouth the next morning. Spread out between the soogans were any extra clothes, and stuffed down at the foot were things that needed washing.

The war sack held all the cowboy's possessions he'd gathered—cigarette makin's, cartridges, letters, playing cards, spare spurs, and such—and served as a lumpy pillow in the absence of anything better.

A cowboy was apt to be mighty attached to his bedroll, because it was as much his home as a house is to us. One ranch tended to get its hands up early and work them until late, and a new hand hired in town allowed he'd be ready to start as soon as he put together a bedroll. A local cowboy who knew the place told him, "Hell, you don't need a bedroll on that spread. Jes' buy yourself a lantern." Likely that was the same ranch that cowboys said was so kind to its hands that it served them two suppers—one way after dark and the other way before sunup.

Bedrolls were carried in the chuck wagon on trail drives. The important role they played in life on the trail was illustrated by what happened during a drive up the Chisholm Trail in 1877. When the herd reached the North Canadian in Indian Territory, the river was up. Crossing swollen streams was not unusual, but what happened next was. "The cattle were started across and were going fine, when it came up a terrific hailstorm, which interrupted the proceedings. One man was across on the other side of the river, naked, with his horse and saddle and about half the herd, and the balance of us were on this side with the other half of the herd and all the supplies. There was no timber on our side of the river, and when the hail began pelting the boys and myself we made a break for the wagon for shelter. We were all naked, and the hail came down so furiously that within a short time it was about two inches deep on the ground. It must have hailed considerably up the river, for the water was so cold we could not get any more of the herd across that day. We were much concerned about getting help to the man across the river. We tried all evening to get one of the boys over, to carry the fellow some clothes and help look after the cattle, but failed in each attempt.... The water was so cold that horse nor man could endure it ... so the man on the other side had to stay over there all night alone and naked.... Next morning everything was lovely and our absent man swam back to us after he had put the cattle in shape. He had a good saddle blanket, which he said had kept him comfortable enough during the night.

"... On the 8th of June, while we were on the Salt Fork, a cold norther blew up, accompanied by rain, and it soon became so cold we had to stop driving about three o'clock in the afternoon and gather wood for the night. We undertook to hold our cattle that night in the open, but it was so cold that we finally drifted them close to the river where there was a little protection, and kept a man on guard to look after them. About daybreak they stampeded, but we soon caught them without loss of a single head. Eight ponies belonging to other herds near us froze to death that night." Bedrolls were mighty popular in country that could get cold enough to freeze horses to death in June.

Women sometimes shared the hardships of the trail. Mrs. Amanda Burks went up the Chisholm Trail in 1871 with her husband's outfit consisting of two herds. "They started in April with about ten cowboys each, mostly Mexicans, and the cooks.... They were only a day out when Marcus Banks, my brother-in-law, came back with a note to me from Mr. Burks asking me to get ready as soon as possible and catch up with the bunch. He also said to bring either Eliza or Nick (black girl and boy who worked for us) to look out for my comfort....

"So Nick and I started in my little buggy drawn by two good brown ponies and overtook the herd in a day's time. Nick, being more skilled than the camp cook, prepared my meals. He also put up my tent evenings, and took it down when we broke up camp.

"... Being springtime, the weather was delightful until we reached Central Texas. Some of the worst electrical and hailstorms I have ever witnessed were in this part and also in North Texas. The lightning seemed to settle on the ground and creep along like something alive....

"On one occasion a prairie fire ran us out of camp before breakfast. We escaped by fleeing to a part of the plain which had been burned before, called 'a burn' by people of that section.

"Two days later my ignorance was the cause of an immense prairie fire. I thought I would build a fire in a gulley while the cook had gone for water. Not later than I had struck the match than the grass all around was in a blaze which spread so quickly that the men could not stop it. They succeeded in beating out the flanks of the fire so that it did not spread out at the sides at the beginning. The fire blazed higher than a house and went straight ahead for fifty miles or more . . . .

"We were three months on the trail when we arrived at Emmet Creek, twenty-two miles from Newton, Kansas.

"We summered here, as did several other Texas ranch men. Market had broken, and everybody that could do so held his cattle hoping for a rise."

The hoped-for rise did not come, and in December the Burks sold their herd and left for sunny Texas, "dressed as if we were Esquimaux, and carrying a bucket of frozen buffalo tongues as a souvenir for my friends in Texas."

While a number of other women followed their men up the Chisholm Trail, and Lizzie Johnson took her own herds to Kansas, one woman trail driver may have been unique. She didn't go up the Chisholm Trail, but her story is worth repeating.

Samuel Dunn Houston was trailing a herd from New Mexico to Colorado when he found himself short-handed and went into Clayton, New Mexico, to try to hire a few hands.

"When I got there I found there were no men in town, but I met an old friend of mine and he told me that there was a kid of a boy around town that wanted to get with a herd and go up the trail, but he had not seen him for an hour or so. I put out to hunt that kid and found him over at the livery stable. I hired him and took him to camp, and put him with the horses and put my rustler with the cattle. I got

along fine for three or four months. The kid would get up the darkest stormy nights and stay with the cattle until the storm was over. He was good natured, very modest, didn't use any cuss words or tobacco, and always pleasant. His name was Willie Matthews, was nineteen years old and weighed one hundred and twenty-five pounds. His home was in Caldwell, Kansas, and I was so pleased with him that I wished many times that I could find two or three more like him.

"Everything went fine until I got to Hugo, Colorado, a little town on the old K.P. Railroad, near the Colorado and Wyoming line. There was good grass and water close to town, so I pulled up about a half a mile that noon and struck camp. After dinner the kid come to where I was sitting and asked me if he could quit. He insisted, said he was homesick, and I had to let him go.

"About sundown we were all sitting around camp and the old herd was coming in on the bed ground. I looked up toward town and saw a lady, all dressed up, coming toward camp, walking. I told the boys we were going to have company. I couldn't imagine why a woman would be coming on foot to a cow camp, but she kept right on coming, and when within fifty feet of camp I got up to be ready to receive my guest. Our eyes were all set on her, and every man holding his breath. When she got up within about twenty feet of me, she began to laugh, and said, 'Mr. Houston, you don't know me, do you?'

"Well, for one minute I couldn't speak. She reached her hand out to me, to shake hands, and I said, 'Kid, is it possible that you are a lady?' That was one time that I could not think of anything to say, for everything that had been said on the old cow trail in the last three or four [months] entered my mind at that moment.

"The kid explained that she had listened to her father, an old-time trail driver from Texas, tell about trail drives many times, 'and I made up my mind that when I was grown I was going up the trail if I had to run off. I had a pony of my own and read in the paper of the big herds passing Clayton, New Mexico, so I said, now is my chance to get on the trail. Not being far over to Clayton, I saddled my pony and told brother I was going out in the country, and I might be gone for a week, but for him to tell papa not to worry about me, I would be back. I had on a suit of brother's clothes and a pair of his boots. In three or four days I was in Clayton looking for a job and I found one. Now, Mr. Houston, I am glad I found you to make the trip with, for I have enjoyed it. I am going just as straight home as I can and that old train can't run too fast for me, when I get on it.'

"The train left Hugo at 11:20 o'clock in the evening. I left one man with the herd and took the kid and every man to town to see the little girl off. I suppose she was the only girl that ever made such a trip as that. She was a perfect lady."

"Willie," or whatever her real name was, was a far cry from the women the cowboys met when they reached Abilene. Of course, after three months on the trail, enduring storms, stampedes, Indians, and just plain boredom, the cowboys were primed for anything when they finally reached the end of the trail, sold the herd, and drew their pay. Some, of course, wound up like the luckless cowpoke in a verse from "The Old Chisholm Trail":

I went to the boss to draw my roll,

He figgered me out nine dollars in the hole.

Others ended the trip with maybe a hundred dollars setting their pockets on fire, in what was to them an exciting town to be explored and enjoyed, and they lost no time in getting down to the business of having what passed for fun.

By the summer of 1870, Abilene had at least seven saloons in addition to the hotel bars. Most of them were in the section of town called Texas Abilene, south of the railroad tracks. The saloons did all they could—not that much effort was needed—to attract the cowboys' business, including adopting names designed to appeal to the Texas crowd: The Alamo, the Lone Star, the Longhorn, the Trail.

Dance halls provided one of the principal modes of entertainment. Joseph McCoy described them as having "wretched music, ground out on dilapidated instruments by beings fully as degraded as the most vile," but cowboys half deaf from the bellowing of longhorn cattle might be excused for not being so critical. Besides, they were not there to listen. "Few more wild, reckless scenes of abandoned debauchery can be seen on the civilized earth than a dance house in full blast in one of the frontier towns," McCoy added. "With the front of his sombrero lifted at an angle of fully forty-five degrees, his huge spurs jangling at every step or motion, his revolvers flapping up and down like a retreating sheep's tail, his eyes lit up from excitement, liquor, and lust, he plunges into it and 'hoes it down' at a terrible rate in the most approved yet awkward country style, often swinging his partner clear off the floor for an entire circle, then 'balance all,' with an occasional demoniac yell near akin to the war whoop of the savage Indian."

Conveniently located to the dance halls was the red-light district, another popular and busy spot for the cowboy to splurge his hard-earned pay. Dubbed the Devil's Half Acre, the hellhole was populated by an aggregation of females variously called sporting women, soiled doves, fallen angels, and other names more descriptive than kind. "Entertainment" was available twenty-four hours a day.

Wicked as Texas Abilene was, the section of nearby Newton called Hide Town was perhaps even worse. "The girls get drunk, shout, swear, and make exhibitions too indecent for description..." a newspaper correspondent said. Exactly what he meant is not clear, but one could suppose that, in keeping with standard practice in the livestock business, the merchandise on sale was available for public inspection prior to delivery. Even well-used as it was, it must have made quite an impression on cowhands fresh from three or four months on the trail during which they had had ample opportunity to inspect the corresponding anatomical parts of many females—all of the cow kind.

Such towns attracted a large number of people whose only object was easy money, and even hell-raising Texas cowboys sometimes found the goings-on a bit much. One recalled dryly, "While we were in Abilene, we found the town was full of all sorts of desperate characters, and I remember one day one of these bad men rode his horse into a saloon, pulled his gun on the bartender, and all quit business. When he came out several others began to shoot up the town. I was not feeling well, so I went over to the hotel to rest, and in a short time the boys of our outfit missed me and instituted a search, finding me at the hotel under a bed."

Hiding under the bed was not necessarily as much cowardly as it was wise.

> "The girls get drunk, shout, swear, and make exhibitions too indecent for description..."

The local newspaper lamented that Abilene had a larger number of cutthroats and desperadoes than any other town of its size on the continent. No less an expert on badmen than gunfighter John Wesley Hardin, who by the end of his career boasted forty notches on his gun, said, "I have seen many fast towns, but Abilene beat them all. The town was filled with sporting men and women, gamblers, cowboys, desperadoes, and the like. It was well supplied with barrooms, hotels, barber shops, and gambling houses; and everything was open." Cowboys visiting Abilene could expect to run into the likes of Ben Thompson, James B. (Wild Bill) Hickok, Hardin, and Phil Coe. Hardin faced Hickok down and refused to surrender his pistols; Coe, a crooked gambler, got into a shooting scrape with Wild Bill and came out the loser.

Hickok impressed badmen with his two silver-mounted, pearl-handled pistols and wowed the ladies with his "graceful, swaying step, squarely set shoulders, well poised head, and fine, firm throat." He dressed in a Prince Albert coat, checkered trousers, and a silk vest embroidered with flowers. He flung a silk-lined cape over his shoulders and wore patent-leather boots with elaborately sewn tops. Able to put ten bullets into one hole in a fence post or shoot a coin out of the air and be damned quick about it, he could handle any trouble Abilene had to offer. Hickok partook of some of the pleasures Abilene had to offer as

well, including a series of mistresses. As other cattle towns sprang up and drained off trade, Abilene declined to the point that he was at last fired, with one day's notice, on grounds that his services were no longer needed. City councils back then must have had considerably more guts than most do today.

Hickok was Abilene's most famous town marshal, but he was not the first. Tom Smith, a former New York City policeman, took the job after several predecessors had been run out of town by rowdy cowboys. No sooner had he pinned on his badge and entered Texas Abilene than a hulk called Big Hank challenged him and refused to surrender his pistol. One blow from Smith's fist laid Big Hank out cold, and word spread that same night that Abilene had a new marshal who meant business. Some still needed convincing, however. The next morning a desperado named Wyoming Frank rode into town and allowed that since he didn't see the marshal, Smith must have heard he was coming and lit out.

Smith came walking down the street, and Wyoming Frank got up in his face, trying to gibe him into a gunfight. Smith didn't play along, insisting that Frank surrender his pistol. Frank didn't like the look he saw in Smith's eyes and started backing up to get room to draw, but Smith matched him step for step, backing him into a saloon already crowded on a Sunday morning. When Frank refused again to give up his weapon, Smith knocked him down, took his pistol, and gave him five minutes to get out of town. The rest of the crowd promptly surrendered their pistols voluntarily. The law had come to Abilene, and everybody knew it.

It is a measure of Abilene's lawlessness that Smith lasted only five months on the job, but ironically, he was not killed by a badman or cowboy but by a local farmer, Andrew McConnell. McConnell had killed a neighbor, and when Smith went to arrest him, McConnell gunned him down and then tried to chop off his head with an axe.

Despite the excesses of Abilene, Dodge City, and the other trail towns, they were aberrations, and the actions of the cowboys while visiting there should be judged in the greater context. Bulah Rust Kirkland, daughter of a man who went up the Chisholm Trail and perhaps

added a verse or two to the song, painted what is probably a balanced picture of the cowboy. "I believe I could walk along the streets of any town or city and pick out the real cowboy, not by his clothes especially, but because one can nearly always notice that he has a very open countenance and almost innocent eyes and mouth. *He is not innocent of course* [emphasis added]; but living in the open, next to nature, the cleaner life is stamped on his face. His vices leave no scars, or few, because old mother nature has him with her most of the time."

A lot of time spent with "old mother nature" and a few raucous hours at the end of the trail shaped the substance of the verses of "The Old Chisholm Trail." Jesse Chisholm brought honor to the name he wore, and the cowboys who traveled the trail and authored the song that also bore it did no less.

～ 2 ～

Fort Griffin

IT COULD BE ARGUED THAT THE HORSE started the whole thing.

Not any particular horse, but "the horse" in the generic sense. Before Europeans arrived in the Americas, various Indian tribes had carved up the country among themselves and established relatively stable territories. In Texas about 1500, Caddoes and Atakapans occupied the Piney Woods of East Texas, Karankawas and Coahuiltecans the Gulf Coast and South Texas, Jumanos the Big Bend country, and Tonkawas and Apaches Central Texas and the Hill Country.

Then the Comanches of Colorado and Wyoming got the horse.

Spanish conquistadors took huge herds of livestock on their expeditions. Cattle and sheep provided food, of course, and horses were for riding. Escapees from the cattle and horse herds remained behind when the expeditions passed on and then multiplied, spreading wide over the plains. After some 200

years, bountiful bands of wild horses roamed the Great Plains, and by 1700 an obscure tribe of Rocky Mountain Indians captured or otherwise acquired some and began to learn their use.

Thus began a reign of terror the like of which North America had never seen before. The Age of the Comanche had dawned. Roy Bedichek said, "The redman and the mustang formed an immediate partnership...and this union shook the life of the Great Plains, human and subhuman, like an earthquake." Before the horse, most Indians seemed to have practiced a combination of gardening (or trading for food with tribes who did) and local hunting. As buffalo herds migrated past, as many were killed as could be used. After the herds were gone, hungry times returned until the animals once again brought a brief spate of plenty.

Horses changed all that. Now the Indians could follow the buffalo no matter how far they roamed, carrying their meager possessions with them. The horse transformed poor, often starving Indians into rich, well-fed lords of the plains who had leisure time enough to develop a splendid culture.

The horse also made the Plains Indians into mobile, wide-ranging killers. Said W. W. Newcomb of the Comanches, "The changes in their culture were revolutionary: from a scrounging, poor, militarily weak rabble, they became in less than a century a mounted, well-equipped, and powerful people." Raids on Spanish settlements replenished the supply of horses. Journeys onto the southern Great Plains after the buffalo led to clashes with the Apaches who had long held the area. By the nineteenth century the Comanches prevailed. They reigned as Lords of the Plains.

War became the dominant way of life of the Comanches. They fought first to gain their hold on the Southern Plains and then to keep their grasp. For nearly 200 years the Comanches warred constantly. To do otherwise would have been to relinquish control of their rich buffalo hunting territory and skulk back to the mountains a defeated, impoverished people.

The Comanches' determination to maintain a better way of life on the land they fought to win brought them into direct conflict with another group of people with the same goal: Texans. A 200-year tradition of winning spurred the Comanches into battle after battle, many of which they won, but the final victory was not to be theirs. Ironically, the horse that propelled them to greatness also carried United States cavalry troopers—principally black buffalo soldiers—and became the instrument of their destruction.

The whites had another trick up their sleeve as well. After Texas became part of the Union in 1845, the United States Army took over responsibility for frontier defense. As settlers spread westward from the Sabine, the military flung out a line of forts a hundred miles or so in advance of the settlements. So rapid was the spread of settlements that the first line of forts—stretching from the Red River to the Rio Grande—was bypassed in a decade. After the Civil War, a second line of forts sprang up farther west. One of them was named Fort Griffin.

* * * * *

Few events have so totally changed a peoples' way of life as did the Comanches' acquisition of the horse. Indians captured descendants of escaped Spanish horses and became what was described as the greatest light cavalry the world has ever seen.

The UT Institute of Texan Cultures at San Antonio, No. 68-127

The Flat - Ft. Griffin

by Michael Stevens
arr. Stevens/Seyer

fin   and   the   hell   hole   it   turned

out   to   be   The

The Flat – Fort Griffin

by Michael Stevens

Gather 'round, I'll tell you a true Texas tale
Laced with pathos, I'm sure you'll agree
On the clear fork of the Brazos, Fort Griffin
And the hell-hole it turned out to be

The army's main mission had a grandiose ring
A string of forts, to protect the frontier
But they failed to deal with the trash that ensued
Their noble plan soon started to queer

First came the young troopers, ahorseback
A tough assignment, this desolate place
And duties, hot, dirty, and boring, could change
In no time, to looking death in the face

Then a city sprung up down in the flats
Its services geared for the need
Of the baser instincts, diversion, and sport
Perpetually fueled by the greed

Lords of the plains, the Comanches, defeated
By McKenzie in the Red River War
At the Battle of Palo Duro Canyon
In 1874

Once again, the flats would prosper and grow
As the buffalo hunters swarmed in
Profits were lewd in lead, powder, and hides
Likewise gamblin', drinkin', and sin

Then the buffalo were gone, we near lost them for good
Guess they thought they outnumbered the stars
Thus went the hunters, for them I don't mourn
And the prairies were littered with the scars

The western trail brought cattle to the railhead at Dodge
To avoid the tick-fever quarantine
Thru Fort Griffin, some claim, toughest town in the west
A haven of the lawless and mean

Fort Griffin and The Flat had one hell of a boom
History teaches most boomers go bust
So when the flag came down and the longhorn drives ceased
It dried up, blew away like their dust

Well, now you have heard my sad, miserable tale
A vignette from the lonely prairie
On the clear fork of the Brazos, Fort Griffin
A state park now, but The Flat you can't see

This view of The Flat below Fort Griffin exaggerates the topography but emphasizes the fact that soldiers at the fort had few options for entertainment.

From The Quirt and the Spur

The older I get the smaller the world becomes. It gets harder and harder to go somewhere and not run into someone I know or who knows someone I know. It's a simple function of age, not popularity.

Actually, there's a mathematical explanation. Someone once figured that if each of us knows a thousand other people by name, you should have to go through no more than three other people to find a connection between yourself and any other person on earth. Multiply it out. A thousand multiplied by itself three times gives a hefty trillion, and at last count there were "only" five billion of us. So actually you should only have to go through a fraction over two other people. I guess that accounts for kids and isolated folks who don't have many acquaintances.

The world was even smaller in Fort Griffin's heyday. One of the neat things about Texas history during the early days is that you keep running into the same people over and over. The cast of characters was small and the stage on which they played was vast, but they managed to cover a lot of ground. People like Wyatt Earp and Doc Holliday and Billy the Kid and Pat Garrett showed up, sooner or later, in lots of places in Texas and neighboring states. They always managed to find their marks on stage center.

All of which goes to point out that although Fort Griffin was just a running sore on the prairie, it attracted—for a time—individuals who, like the town they visited, played parts in a larger drama. The story of Fort Griffin is just one of many subplots in the epic of Texas history. (As Shakespeare put it, "All the world's a stage, And all the men and women merely players. They have their exits and their entrances, And one man in his time plays many parts.")

In one sense, though, Fort Griffin's story is the saga of the taming of Texas—for better or for worse—in microcosm. Actors who pranced across Fort Griffin's stage included Native Americans, soldiers, buffalo hunters, outlaws, lawmen, rustlers, gamblers, lewd women, mysterious characters, and other assorted types. A wild country was subdued, settled, and secured. The people were raw, rough, and seldom repentant. As such they reflected the elements against which they struggled and the times in which they lived. They are not ours to judge or condemn, but simply to acknowledge as having once been among us. Their seeds lie dormant in us still.

Fort Griffin

Texas frontier forts defied the popular notion of stockaded enclosures with imposing walls of upright logs sharpened at the top. In the first place, timber was usually not available to build such structures. A cartoon once sat on the park ranger's desk at Fort Lancaster on the Pecos River in West Texas. It showed two mounted Indians sitting on a treeless hill overlooking a log-walled fort in the treeless valley below. One Indian was saying to the other, "What I want to know is, where did they get all those trees?"

Secondly, Texas frontier forts were not built for defensive purposes. They were living quarters from whence the troops went out on patrol. At first the army sent infantry to pursue the Indians, with little success. Then Fort Mason was chosen to carry out an experiment. Hand-picked men and horses made up a cavalry post. Troops commanded by the likes of Robert E. Lee and John Bell Hood demonstrated the superior effectiveness of cavalry against the Indians, and after the Civil War, cavalry was the weapon of choice against the Indians, who were themselves among the finest light cavalry the world has yet seen.

Fort Griffin was located on the Clear Fork of the Brazos in what is now Shackelford County, about 15 miles north of present-day Albany. At the time of its founding in 1867, the area was on the extreme western frontier, and Indian raids had recently resulted in the deaths of dozens of local citizens.

Unlike frontier forts such as Fort Davis, Fort Griffin was not substantially built. A few buildings were of stone, but as the post surgeon pointed out in a report in 1867, most were not. "The fort is built entirely of wood and the lumber, from which the buildings were constructed, was sawed in the mill, put up by the fort quartermaster in the neighborhood, and being green at the time it was worked up, the boards have warped and shrunk to such an extent in some instances as to cause many buildings to leak badly."

Fort Griffin quickly developed a reputation as the armpit of the army. Sanitation was often ignored. Trash collected in ravines and on hillsides. Not all of it was removed from camp. A newly arrived fort surgeon in 1870 had to build a new storeroom because the existing one was so filled with trash, and when he went to clean the old one, he found he might better have just burned it down. "Two fire buckets were found containing—in a state of decomposition—one specimen of a portion of the entrails of some beef cattle, the other human being...."

The unsavory character of the army post was not enhanced by the civilian settlement that grew up in the Brazos River bottom below the post, which sat on a slight elevation. The flat had been rejected by the military, but others were not so choosy.

It has been said that an army fights on its stomach, but it could as easily be said of troops of the late 1800s that they rested on their libidos. Settlements catering to the troopers' baser instincts sprang up around military posts and were generally officially decried and unofficially winked at. The Flat at Fort Griffin is generally acknowledged as having been the equal of any such town in its depravity and violence.

The Flat offered the soldiers at Fort Griffin prostitution, gambling, drinking, and gun fighting. Prostitutes often operated under the guise of laundresses, but the laundry service was simply a way for the government to tolerate prostitution. Other unsavory characters dedicated to the proposition that the only good soldier was a fleeced soldier moved in to establish saloons and gambling houses. They prospered.

Fort Griffin and the Flat reached new depths after the Comanches were defeated in the Red River War in 1874. Cavalry troops under Ranald Mackenzie caught the main band of Comanches in Palo Duro Canyon and dealt them a stinging defeat. Almost the entire horse herd of the Indians was captured and killed. As the Comanches had sown, so did they reap. Once afoot, they ceased to be the Lords of the Plains and became instead almost defenseless. Soon most straggled into Oklahoma reservations and surrendered.

The defeat of the Comanches opened the way for buffalo hunters to send the southern herd of buffalo into oblivion as they had already done the northern. Fort Worth offered rail services to ship the hides east. In the middle, between the buffalo hunting grounds to the west and the railroad terminus to the east, was Fort Griffin. The Flat became the chief supply point and recreational arena for hundreds of buffalo hunters. As money flowed, it attracted all those classes of people who would become rich without working, and the Flat moved to a higher plane of iniquity.

The merchant firm of Conrad and Rath furnishes a gauge of how active commerce was at this time. The firm bought buffalo hides and sold the hunters supplies, making money both ways. The store stocked 30 tons of lead and 5 tons of powder, and as much as $4,000 a day changed hands across its counters.

Buffalo hunting was not a pretty business. Buffalo hunter John R. Cook described it matter-of-factly but with a tinge of remorse. "Arriving on the breaks of the Salt Fork of the Brazos River, we realized that we were in the midst of that vast sea of animals that caused us gladness and sorrow, joy, trouble and anxiety,

Both Indians and whites knew the slaughter of the buffalo sounded the death knell for the Indians' wild, free way of life. Killing without caring or conscience, some hunters took only the tongues, leaving the rest for the coyotes and buzzards.

The UT Institute of Texan Cultures at San Antonio, No. 73-1564

but independence, for the succeeding years....

"Too late to stop and moralize now. And sentiment must have no part in our thoughts from this time on. We must have these 3361 hides that this region is to furnish us inside of three months, within a radius of eight miles from this main camp. So at it we went. And Hart... started out, and in two hours had killed sixty-three bison.

"...It was now a busy time. Some days thirty and forty-odd hides, then a good day with eighty-five, and one day in February, one hundred and seventy-one; then again the same month, 203; and these 203 were killed on less than ten acres of ground....

"We had good hunting at this camp until the last of February, when all at once the buffalo were not to be seen....

"We then had stacked up and drying 2003 hides; 902 of them I had skinned, and was so accredited. This was an average of 22 buffaloes a day for 41 days. At 25 cents per hide I had earned $225.50....

"...I learned that a man named Hickey was at [Fort] Griffin as agent for Loganstein and Company, of Leavenworth, Kansas, with instructions to buy all the buffalo-hides offered for sale; to pay for them on the range and haul them to Fort Worth, Texas, with freight teams....

"Mr. Hickey arrived at our camp late in the afternoon, and found everybody present. Not a buffalo had been seen that day.

"The next morning Charlie and Hickey went to the first camp. Mr. Hickey made some little examination of the hides, and they returned. A satisfactory deal had been made between them. He gave Charlie a check for $2,000, and agreed to pay the balance as soon as the hides reached Fort Griffin.... So it was arranged that they would all go to Fort Griffin, where Charlie would get his check cashed and settle up in full with all of them....

"The next morning they all pulled out for Griffin. I was left alone....

"As Charlie bade me good-by, he being the last one to leave the camp, he said he would be back in six days.... To make a long story short, Charlie was twenty-one days getting back to camp. But he had had a glorious spree. He got his check cashed at the post sutler's; paid all the boys up, and deposited all that was coming to me with the sutler, taking his receipt for it....

"He said, 'I never intended to get drunk; but what could a fellow do? There were about thirty outfits camped on the Clear Fork of the Brazos, under big pecan trees, and we all had a time....'"

As squalid as it was, Fort Griffin offered a diversion from the weeks on the plains spent killing and skinning buffalo, and the hunters took full advantage. The Flat had saloons, soiled doves, and dance halls in plenty, and moral restraints were few. "I've seen men and women dancing there in the dance halls without a bit of clothing on," one hunter recalled. Another hunter sold his season's hides for $1,500 one day and had to borrow money for breakfast the next, having made a donation to the gambler's welfare society in the meantime. Those the gamblers could not cheat in crooked games, they got drunk and rolled in the alleys.

Despite the preponderance of establishments geared to the sating of carnal appetites, Fort Griffin served as an important supply point for the Texas frontier. Early businesses catered to soldiers and buffalo hunters. Later came cowboys trailing herds up the Western Trail to Dodge City, Kansas. All required a variety of services and merchandise, and where demand exists, supply will follow. The town on the Flat grew up helter-skelter as stores one after another were thrown up.

One early resident described the result: "The one long street, from the foot of the hill through the town to the crossing of the Clear Fork, was alive with men and horses and in many places near the supply stores wagons were jammed together in a way that almost stopped travel. . . .

"It was the palmy days of Fort Griffin, when money flowed like water through the avenues of businesses, and men handled it with the same careless indifference that merchants handled bacon, flour and potatoes. Not hundreds but thousands of dollars changed hands each day. And one day spent in the Flat, and one night among the denizens who frequented the resorts, would convince any man that it was not a question of price, but whether the supply would hold out."

Until Shackelford County was organized in 1874, the Flat remained under the nominal jurisdiction of the commander of Fort Griffin. However, once the county was formed, civilian authorities took over—or at least, that was the theory. In reality, the Flat became even more of a hellhole than before, since law existed in name only. Gunfighters such as Wyatt Earp, Doc Holliday, Pat Garrett, and John Selman rubbed elbows with what respectable element there was, and for a time Fort Griffin was undoubtedly the "toughest town in the west."

Female inhabitants of the Flat were referred to in polite society as soiled doves, fallen angels, frail sisters, damsels of spotted virtue, and the like. However, the names appended to them by their customers were less kind and more descriptive: Big Nose Kate, Hurricane Minnie, Long Kate, and (in other locales) Gizzard Lip Sue, Rocking Chair Annie, and so on. The women conducted the public part of their business in the saloons and the private part in shanties sprawled along the riverbank.

Upwards of a dozen saloons operated in the Flat. Chief among them was the Bee Hive, which had this sign painted on the front:

Within this hive we are all alive,
Good whiskey makes us funny,
If you are dry step in and try
the essence of our honey.

Activities in the saloons and riverbank shanties were illegal, and cases were filed in district court against the offending parties. Long Kate and Hurricane Minnie were charged with fighting in a grocery store. Along with others, they were also charged with "keeping a disorderly house, to wit: a house where vagabonds & prostitutes resort for the purpose of public prostitution." Thomas Grise and Isaac Blum were charged with "permitting diverse persons to play at a game with cards with each other in a house under their control & when used by them for retailing spiritous liquors."

Such charges appear to have been filed more for the purpose of generating revenue for the county than for curtailing the illegal activities. In most cases charges were simply allowed to accumulate, and once a year the offending parties were brought into court, fined $100 on each count, and promptly released. The system seems to have taken the place of an occupation tax; the fines were more or less a license to operate. In return for paying a fine once a year, the frail sisters were left to operate in peace the rest of the time.

In contrast, truly serious violations of the law were often winked at. One man rode into town, tied up his horse at a hitching rack, and proceeded to get drunk. After standing at the hitching post all day and the following night, the horse was beginning to suffer from thirst. A Tonkawa Indian who lived nearby untied the horse and started to lead him to water. The drunken owner shot the Indian dead, bellowing that he would take care of his own horse. He was jailed until he sobered up, and that was the end of the matter—until the man turned up dead a few weeks later of an "accidental" gunshot wound. Some said John Selman, a local gunslinger, had avenged the death of his Indian friend.

Hurricane Bill Martin, a horse thief and cheater at cards, had a run-in with Mike O'Brien at the Bee Hive Saloon. Neither was armed, and both dashed off to find a weapon to settle their quarrel. Mike reached his first—a heavy .50-caliber buffalo gun—and began firing at Bill, who took refuge in a shanty across the street. Mike sat down in the middle of the street and began reducing the shanty to splinters while Bill dodged bullets and tried to shoot back. As the whole town turned out to watch, one of Mike's friends took him a bottle of liquor to steady his nerves. After he ran out of booze and bullets, Mike returned to the saloon, and the whole affair was soon forgotten.

Black troopers from the fort became embroiled in many of the shootings and fights. In spite of a record of bravery and discipline that exceeded that of white troops of the time, the buffalo soldiers were not immune to the temptations of the Flat, and they were discriminated against then as surely as they would be for the next hundred years.

On one occasion the white troopers at Fort Griffin were given passes into town and the black troopers were not. The blacks decided they would go to town as well, passes or not. The post guard ordered them to stop or be shot, and the troopers returned to their barracks and got their weapons. The guard backed down and let them go to town, where they were met by Texas Ranger captain G. W. Arrington and some seventy white troopers. The blacks refused to obey the order of the lieutenant in charge of the troopers to go back to the fort, but Captain Arrington succeeded in getting them to do so.

At times trouble sought out the black troops. In October 1876 a drunken buffalo hunter burst into the mess hall with a pistol in each hand and ordered the soldiers to leave. Then he threatened to kill any who tried to return. The company captain ordered a detail to kill the hunter and retake the hall, but before they could act, the local sheriff, John Larn, talked the hunter out and took him back to the Flat. There he put the drunk in a vacant shack to sleep it off and wedged the door shut with a log. However, the hunter tore up some floorboards and started a fire to keep warm, setting the whole place on fire. Unable to get out because of the log holding the door, the hunter nearly died from smoke inhalation before the sheriff arrived and rescued him. Now sober, the hunter was released.

The Flat was home—for a short while —to a number of colorful characters. Outstanding among them was Lottie Deno, not your average soiled dove. Other damsels of spotted virtue might be found swilling booze in saloons, swearing or fighting on the street, or plying their trade in public view, but not Lottie Deno. Lottie's virtue was unquestioned—like all the others, she was a whore—but she carried on her occupation with style. She dressed well, was never seen drinking, and did not consort with the lewd women of the Flat.

Much of Lottie Deno's fame arose from the fact that she kept pretty much to herself and never revealed anything of her background. Fort Griffin gossips loved having a genuine mystery woman to talk about, and all kinds of stories circulated about her. One said she was a wronged wife. Another held that she became a gambler to try to regain a family fortune swept away by the Civil War. Still another said she worked to support an invalid mother. But the truth was that nobody knew, then or now, any more about Lottie Deno's past than she chose to reveal, and that was precious little.

Lottie became the mistress of one Shannessy, a local saloon owner, and she regularly gambled in his establishment. She was certainly no angel, but in comparison with the other female residents of the Flat she was almost saintly, and she pretty much stayed out of trouble until Johnny Golden showed up.

No one ever knew whether Golden and Deno had known each other earlier, but Sheriff John Jacobs thought so. He said Lottie told him that Golden knew her husband's troubles and she had to keep him pacified. At any rate, Deno dumped Shannessy and became Golden's girl. Enraged, Shannessy hired two hit men, and no better illustration of the state of law enforcement in Fort Griffin is needed than the fact that his hired killers were deputy sheriff Jim Draper and town marshal Bill Gilson. The two arrested Golden in Shannessy's, charging him with horse stealing despite his claim he had never owned a horse. The next day his body was found on the ground with a bullet hole beneath it—he had been knocked down and shot while on the ground. The two lawmen concocted a variety of stories to explain Golden's death, none of which were believable. Nevertheless, the local justice of the peace cleared them.

Lottie grieved over Golden's death, paid for his funeral, and withdrew from public view. While she did not attend his funeral service, murderer Bill Gilson did. After a month of living in her shanty, having supplies brought to her, Lottie left town on the stage, unannounced. When her room was finally opened, a note was said to have been found that said, "Sell this outfit and give the money to someone in need of assistance." That was the end of Lottie Deno. No one knows what happened to her, although one story says she later turned up in New Mexico under another name, married, became a churchgoer and doer of good, and died in 1934 at age eighty at which time a glowing obituary told of her good deeds.

When law did finally come to Fort Griffin, it was a mixed blessing. A man tough enough to handle the drunken buffalo hunters and rowdy trail drovers on the Flat was himself likely to have a violent and sometimes unlawful past. John Larn was elected sheriff in 1876 and chose John Selman as his deputy.

Larn and Selman were active in ridding the Flat of undesirables, but they apparently did not do so alone or in strict observance of the law. To the contrary, Larn seems to have at least condoned, if not assisted, the activities of a local vigilance committee that referred to itself as the Old Law Mob or the Tin-Hat Brigade. Edgar Rye, the justice of the peace, explained the blind eye that was turned to the lynchings the Old Law Mob regularly held. "When it is understood that the honest, legitimate citizens were in the minority and scattered over a large area, while the thieves, robbers and murderers were banded together and did not hesitate to testify falsely in court or waylay and kill witnesses to prevent conviction, the necessity to organize a Vigilance Committee to rid the community of these lawless characters when the law was impotent, at once becomes apparent."

Barely ten days after Larn was elected sheriff, lynch law took over at Fort Griffin. Houston Faught was shot when caught horse stealing. Taken to the post hospital for treatment, Faught was abducted by masked riders, taken to the bank of the Clear Fork, and hanged. The editor of the Jacksboro *Frontier Echo* commented, "...it seems as though no medicine will reach the case but blue whistlers [bullets] or hemp.... The people have risen in their might and declared that thieves shall no longer rule the country."

Soon three more bad-men swung from trees along the Clear Fork, near the shanty of Indian Kate. Sheriff Larn brought two others in and jailed them in Albany. The next night a mob took them and hanged them. Typical of the time was the treat-ment of a horse thief as reported in the *Echo* in a dispatch from Fort Griffin: "The notorious character known as 'Reddy' of horse thief fame, was captured on the 2nd inst. at this place for horse stealing in Eastland county, and put in the military guardhouse for safe keeping.

"On Friday afternoon he was turned over to parties to be conveyed to Eastland county. Yesterday his body was found hanging to a tree three miles from here."

"...it seems as though no medicine will reach the case but blue whistlers [bullets] or hemp.... The people have risen in their might and declared that thieves shall no longer rule the country."

Lynchings were numerous during Larn's stint as sheriff, after which he returned to his area ranch. In a fitting end, he himself was soon sent to per-dition by Judge Lynch. Larn formed a partnership with John Selman, and the two surrounded themselves with a gang of toughs. Larn and Selman obtained a contract to furnish three beeves a day for the troops at Fort Griffin. They made reg-ular deliveries—of other people's cattle. Soon a warrant was issued for their arrest, and Texas Rangers formed a posse for the purpose. The men were taken into custody at Larn's ranch; fresh cowhides, none with Larn's brand, were fished out of the river below his house; yet when the two appeared in court in Fort Griffin, they were released.

Larn and Selman now believed they were above the law, and they proceeded to attempt to eliminate their enemies. Riding at night, they began to steal cattle and murder their owners. Small ranchers and farmers became so terrified they left their crops to fend for themselves and would not leave their houses, sending their wives out to do any necessary errands. Shortly Larn and Selman made the first of two fatal mis-takes: They shot a victim and let him get away. The farmer, a man named A. J.

Lancaster, went to Albany and swore out a complaint against Larn, Selman, and other members of their gang.

When he and eleven of his followers were arrested, Larn made the mistake that sealed his fate. He told the members of the posse that took him in that if he escaped, they were all dead men. Selman, meanwhile, hearing of Larn's arrest, took off. Larn and his gang were jailed in Albany, and when night came, an eerie silence settled on the town. No one walked the streets. People shuttered their houses and huddled inside. Everyone —including John Larn—knew what was going to happen.

Around one or two in the morning some thirty-five masked men quietly surrounded the Albany jail. The four guards on duty were quickly disarmed. Some ten or fifteen men crowded into the room where Larn and the others were chained together in leg irons. Seconds later Larn lay dead of nine bullet wounds.

John Selman made it as far as Fort Davis in West Texas, where he was soon jailed for his misdeeds there. Returned to Albany by Texas Rangers, he was given a horse by the local sheriff and told to get out and never come back. He ended his career in El Paso eighteen years later. In 1895 he killed John Wesley Hardin in a saloon, and less than a year later was gunned down himself by a U.S. marshal.

At the time Larn was dying, the Flat was, too, but it had one last chance to milk the pockets of passers-through. As soldiers forced the Indians onto reservations and buffalo hunters wiped out the herds roaming the plains, ranchers saw in the sea of grass an opportunity. Millions of longhorns were moved north not only to feed the hungry mouths of Northern factory workers but also to stock the now-empty range.

Texas cattle did have a problem: They were disease carriers. Tick fever, a disease to which the longhorns were immune but which they carried, followed the herds. Kansas passed laws quarantining portions of the state, first in the east and then farther west. Trail drives were pushed steadily westward to keep Texas cattle away from Kansas stock. By 1876 the only legal railhead available to Texas cattle was Dodge City, which was due north of Fort Griffin. The Western Trail developed, and merchants on the Flat switched from supplying buffalo hunters to outfitting cattle drovers. The money from both spent the same.

Fort Griffin became a supply point that rivaled Fort Worth, on the Chisholm Trail farther east. Fort Griffin merchants sent representatives to Belton, on the Chisholm Trail, to persuade drovers to trail their herd through Fort Griffin. They met with considerable success, and for several years the number of cattle trailed through Fort Griffin greatly exceeded the number passing through Fort Worth.

Just about the time cowboys started to hit the Flat in large numbers, respectability was rearing its genteel head in Fort Griffin. A warning to cowboys in the *Echo* in 1879 gave a good picture of what went on as well as how locals regarded the events.

"After spending weeks and often months on the range, a natural desire takes possession of many of you, to visit town, shave, clean up, put on new clothes, get 'biling drunk,' fire your six-shooter and raise the devil generally....

"Our citizens are always glad to see you come to town but they do not like to see you get into rows or disturb the peace.

"...Come to town as often as you want to, boys, stay as long and drink as much mean whisky as you can and enjoy yourselves in any way you please, but do not do those things which you know are likely to make trouble for yourselves."

Visits to town, themselves rowdy, often wound up with a final binge of exuberant gunplay. One outfit prepared to leave town early one morning after having spent all night debauching in the saloons. Dick Bell, the outfit's black cook, rode in to tell the cowboys the herd was ready to move, and they mounted their horses to bid the Flat farewell in the usual style, by galloping through town firing their pistols. A deputy sheriff and three others hid in bushes near the edge of town, but the cowboys took another trail. Bell followed seconds later and stuck to the main road, and the posse threw down on him and called for him to surrender.

Bell blasted away with his pistol and headed back toward town, where a shot felled his horse. Bullets continued to fly until Bell was wounded eleven times and gave up the fight. Within two weeks he was back on the trail.

Fort Griffin and the nearby Flat were boomers, and like most such, they also became busters. The soldiers and the buffalo and the longhorns faded away in time, and there was nothing to replace them. The buffalo were shot out by 1878; the flag was lowered at the fort the last time on May 31, 1881; by 1882 barbed wire spelled the end to the open range and the big drives. The Flat at last lived up to its name and went busted.

Today the Texas Parks and Wildlife Department maintains Fort Griffin State Historical Park among the ruins of the military post, but virtually nothing remains of the Flat. Perhaps what I once heard an archeologist expound on at length is relevant. After four days of hard digging at a supposed Indian site during which absolutely nothing was found—not even one flint chip—he proposed the theory that he had obviously discovered the location of the one Indian activity of which there would be no material remains: a brothel.

Comedian Red Buttons became quite well known at one time for a routine he performed at various celebrity roasts during which he would question why the honoree got a dinner when so many other more-deserving individuals—according to him—never did. The same question could perhaps be asked about Fort Griffin. Why did the Chisholm Trail get a song, but not Fort Griffin? Why did Abilene and Amarillo get a song, but not Fort Griffin?

The answer, obviously, is that nobody ever wrote a song for Fort Griffin. Michael Stevens corrected that oversight. The words and the music are his. The memories they rouse belong to all.

❦ 3 ❧

Streets of Laredo

WHAT DO A GUNSHOT COWBOY IN Laredo, an English hospital, and a soldier dying of syphilis have in common?

This is not a sick joke.

The answer is, all share the same ancestral tune. "Streets of Laredo" is descended directly from an eighteenth-century English ballad, "The Unfortunate Rake," which told the sad life story of an English soldier who had been infected by a young lady of his casual acquaintance. The lad lay dying in St. James Hospital in London, later to be known as St. James Infirmary, and that is how the title of the blues classic "St. James Infirmary" came about.

The theme of a not-so-innocent but misfortunate young man cut down in his prime who counsels others not to follow in his footsteps had enormous appeal. The song was probably brought to America by people moving here from England, and their descendants carried it westward, adapting the content to fit the times in which they lived. The song's protagonist (or agonist, if you will) varied from place to place and time to time. There were trooper, sailor, and good-girl-gone-wrong versions. The scene of the dying cowboy's tragedy was placed in Dodge City and Galveston as well as Laredo. Even the title sometimes changed to "The Cowboy's Lament."

"Streets of Laredo" is perhaps the premiere example of both cowboy and folk songs. It has evolved, it has endured, and it still retains its power to evoke powerful emotions in the listener.

* * * * *

The Streets of Laredo

Trad.
arr. Stevens/Seyer

As I walked out in the streets of Laredo
As I walked out in Laredo one day
I spied a young cowboy all dressed in white linen
Wrapped in white linen as cold as the clay

I see by your outfit that you are a cowboy
These words he did say as I boldly stepped by
Come sit here beside me and hear my sad story
Oh I'm a young cowboy and I know I must die

'Twas was once in the saddle I used to go dashin'
It was once in the saddle I used to go gay
First to the dram-house then to the card-house
Got shot in the breast and I'm dying today

Get six jolly cowboys to carry my coffin
Get six pretty maidens to bear up my pall
Put bunches of roses all over my coffin
To deaden the sound of the clods as they fall

Now bring me a drink a drink of cool water
To cool my parched lips the poor cowboy said
But before I returned the spirit had left him
And gone to his master the cowboy was dead

So we beat the drum slowly we played the fife lowly
And played the dead march as we carried him along
For we all loved our comrade so brave young and handsome
We all loved our comrade although he'd done wrong

How the cowboy in the song met his fatal bullet can only be conjectured. Along the Texas-Mexico border in the last quarter of the nineteenth century, the possible ways were many.

It is difficult for people living today along the I-35 corridor from Dallas to Waco to Austin to Laredo to realize that in 1865, this was the frontier. Beyond, where the uplifted edge of the Balcones Escarpment rose away in broken hills, was a vast territory teeming with game, wild cattle, and Indians. A few restless settlers had pushed into the region and warred with the Indians for control; the issue was still very much in doubt. Comanches, Apaches, and Kiowas regarded settlements in Texas and Mexico as their "ranchos," devoted to raising cattle and horses which the Indians "cropped" on annual raids.

The end of the Civil War brought home thousands of men defeated in battle but not in spirit, accustomed to killing, and destitute. Most got about the business of putting their lives back together by legal means. They married, started families, plowed fields, clerked in stores, chased cattle, did the thousand civilized things their chivalrous upbringing and their Southern mamas had prepared them to do.

Others took a different road.

Texas was a lawless land after the Civil War. A corrupt Reconstruction government aggravated feelings already inflamed by war and defeat, and many people openly defied civil authority. Some did so out of principle, others out of convenience or avarice. Conflicts such as the Mason County War and the Horrell-Higgins Feud developed into small-scale wars. Men who lived by the gun were attracted to an atmosphere where what law there was had more than it could handle trying to keep supposedly decent people from murdering each other.

Between the Nueces and the Rio Grande was the worst of all the outlaw nests in Texas. The area had been thinly settled in the mid-1700s by Hispanic ranchers who gave birth to the ranching tradition now so closely identified with Texas. Between the Texas Revolution of 1836 and the end of the Mexican War in 1848, the region was in limbo. Mexico claimed the boundary between Texas and Mexico was the Nueces; Texas claimed the Rio Grande as the line. Neither side exercised strong authority over the region, which extended from Brownsville to El Paso. Law-abiding citizens who managed to survive in the area did so by living in fortresses and fighting off Indians and outlaws.

Following the Mexican War, Anglo marauders dispossessed many of the Hispanic landowners. Mexicans were classed with Indians as subhuman forms of life that had to be eradicated before the country could be "civilized." Racial prejudice was nowhere stronger in Texas than here, where a man whose skin was brown could be killed for no reason and no questions were asked. Cattle stealing was a way of life. Anglo outlaws joined forces with Mexican nationalists in driving Texas cattle south of the Rio Grande.

Into this seething cauldron of iniquity rode the Texas Rangers.

The name *ranger* is derived from loosely organized companies of men authorized by Stephen F. Austin to guard the frontier of his colony in the 1820s. These "ranging companies" were enlisted for short periods of time to scout for Indians and make punitive raids against them. During the troubles with Mexico leading to the Texas Revolution, the first official corps of Texas Rangers was formed. Among the first ranger leaders was Silas Parker, father of Cynthia Ann.

Much has been written pro and con about the Texas Rangers. To some they were the epitome of virtuous manhood and bravery. To others they were ruthless killers who trampled civil rights under booted and spurred heels. No doubt they were some of each. Their personal survival demanded they be so. They had to be badder than the badmen they fought.

Perhaps it was a Texas Ranger who put the bullet in the breast of the dying cowboy in "Streets of Laredo." Or, a ranger may have brought the cowboy's slayer to justice—or, equally likely, killed him in the attempt. Whatever the case, the "Streets of Laredo" could well have been the theme song of the Texas Rangers, telling as it does the violent end to a life gone wrong.

The dying cowboy in "Streets of Laredo" was *e pluribus unum*. As a law-enforcement body, the Texas Rangers were, in contrast, one of a kind. Heroes to some and devils to others, the Texas Rangers nevertheless did what they saw as right, and they kept on a-comin' until their kind was no longer needed.

Streets of Laredo

Laredo has a long, proud history not even hinted of in the song. The town was founded in 1755 by José de Escandón, who has been described as the last conquistador and the first empresario. The title is fitting, as he not only conquered a vast wilderness but also peopled it. He established more than a dozen settlements along the Rio Grande, and Laredo was the last.

Livestock multiplied rapidly on the pastures along the Rio Grande, and the Spanish crown allotted lands to the settlers for ranching. The little town of Laredo was also laid out, in the Spanish fashion, according to a plan. A central plaza formed the town center, with the east side reserved for the church and the west side for municipal buildings. The little square and the narrow streets laid out by the Spanish still anchor downtown Laredo.

After the Texans won their independence in 1836, a number of expeditions tried to extend control over the disputed territory between the Nueces and the Rio Grande. While these met with limited success, they did keep the region in turmoil. Further upset sprang from political upheaval in Mexico. The northern provinces of Mexico, far from the authorities in Mexico City, proved to be hotbeds of revolution. Soldiers fought for a return to the same Constitution of 1824 the Texans at the Alamo had championed.

In 1840 Laredo became the capital of the short-lived Republic of the Rio Grande, a union of the states of Tamaulipas, Nuevo León, and Coahuila. In keeping with Mexican claims, the territory of the fledgling republic included the land between the Rio Grande and the Nueces. The building which served as the republic's capitol still stands on the south side of San Agustín Square in downtown Laredo.

Many Texans supported the Republic of the Rio Grande, either hoping it would serve as a buffer between the fledgling republic and Mexico or thinking they might take over the new, weak territory themselves. This earned them once more the enmity of the federal government of Mexico. When the Republic of the Rio Grande's tiny army was defeated and the republic ended after less than a year, the victorious Mexicans pledged "Peace! Peace! eternal peace among Mexicans! War, war, eternal war against Texans and the barbarous Comanches!"

The Texans had a knack for making everybody mad at them. Not only were the Mexicans out to get Texans, but the Comanches were, too—and with good reason. In 1840, while Texas was an independent nation, Texans invited all the

Texas Rangers in the late 1800s were armed with more than guns: They had the determination to "Keep on comin'."

Texas Department of Public Safety

Comanche chiefs to come to a meeting in San Antonio for peace talks.

The Texans engaged in a bit of subterfuge that backfired. Once they had the chiefs inside the meeting room, they announced that the Indians would be held prisoner until all white captives were returned. Fighting broke out when the chiefs attempted to free themselves, and thirty-five Indians were killed, eight wounded, and twenty-nine captured. The Texans' treachery turned the Comanches against them forever. For the next forty years the Comanches made war on Texans and refused to treat with them.

A few vignettes from Ranger battles with Indians will illustrate their methods and the results they obtained.

1843. The Texas Rangers were among the first to realize that Comanche arms were superior to the white man's in a close fight. Single-shot muzzle-loading rifles and pistols were cumbersome and took up to a minute to reload. In the time it took to fire one shot and reload, a Comanche could shower tens of arrows on an opponent.

The rangers needed more firepower, and they got it in Samuel Colt's repeating revolvers. Although the cylinders of the first models still had to be loaded in the fashion of a muzzle-loader, they did hold five shots instead of one, and the rangers equipped themselves with a spare cylinder for each gun. Thus, a ranger equipped with the usual two single-shot pistols, two revolvers, and a rifle had twenty-three rounds available to be fired before reloading.

Jack Hays and fifteen rangers were the first to demonstrate to the Comanches what this additional firepower meant in a battle. The Comanches didn't like what they learned. While out on a scout northwest of San Antonio, Hays and his men were surprised by perhaps two to three hundred Indians. The rangers took refuge in a thicket, and the Indians charged, taking pistol fire as they came. The warriors rode out of pistol range, reformed, and drew the rifle fire of the rangers. Thinking that now all their foes would be reloading, the Comanches charged again. To their surprise and horror, the rangers rose from the thicket with a Colt revolver in each hand thundering and smoking—again, again, and again. Indian bodies littered the ground.

The Comanches withdrew to confer, trying to figure out what had just happened to them. Hays didn't give them time to do so. He and his men spun spare cylinders into their revolvers and charged. Hays and nine others drove through the Comanche line, turned, and rode through them again, a blazing pistol in each hand and the reins in their teeth. The chief fell, and the rest began to withdraw, wailing in lamentation over the loss of so many of their comrades. Hays led another charge to hasten them on their way. They left scores of dead behind; eight rangers were wounded.

1844. Results were similar in a battle on the Nueces. Charged by two hundred warriors, the rangers waited until the Indians were on them before firing—and then the hail of lead kept on, and on. Fighting at such close quarters, the spitting fire from their revolvers scorched the Indians' hides, and the rangers panicked the much larger force. The chief leading the Indians later said he never wanted to fight "Devil Yack" again: "Every one of his men had as many shots as I have fingers on my two hands. I lost half of my warriors in the battle, and many others died along the route when returning to my country. . . . "

Another Comanche chief lost his life in a battle that was later immortalized in engraving on the cylinders of Colt's repeating pistols. Once again Hays charged a superior force and routed it with the help of the Colt revolvers. The rangers killed and wounded over fifty Indians while losing one dead and four wounded. So effective was the ranger fire from the pistols that the casualties on the Indians were inflicted by no more than 150 shots.

It fell to the Texans Rangers to deal with not only raiding Indians but also with Mexican bandits and common outlaws. They fell to their work with a will and, in the Texas tradition, bruised a lot of feelings in doing so. A lot of young men died on the streets of Laredo and other towns before the rangers finished their work.

The rangers forged a reputation for blood-thirsty hatred of Mexicans during the Mexican War. Led by legendary leaders such as Samuel H. Walker and John Coffee ("Jack") Hays, the rangers terrorized the Mexicans. When victorious American forces entered Mexico City, the residents flocked to see the rangers they called *Los Diablos Tejanos*—The Texas Devils.

The rangers soon demonstrated that the name was well deserved. When one of their number was murdered in the streets of the city, the rangers went on a rampage. They roamed the streets killing indiscriminately. More than eighty Mexicans were gunned down in the streets and left lying. General Winfield Scott, commanding general of the army, called Jack Hays on the carpet. Hays told the general no one could tell the rangers what to do, and that was the end of the matter. This attitude of being somehow above the law while charged with enforcing it explains much about the fear rangers engendered in lawbreakers, the hatred Mexicans felt for them, and the effectiveness with which they operated.

George Durham was a member of Captain Leander McNelly's force that operated between the Nueces and the Rio Grande in the 1870s. He recalled McNelly's instructions on dealing with the public. "There are only two kinds of people for us—outlaws and law-abiding," McNelly said. "Treat these law-abiding folks with all respect, regardless of color

This caricature of an early Texas Ranger with rifle, Bowie knife, four pistols, and bottle of liquor at the ready is not totally inaccurate; rangers of the time were described as "a desperate set of fellows" whose survival depended on the rule "do unto others before they do it unto you."

The UT Institute of Texan Cultures at San Antonio, No. 73-1316

or size. Don't enter a house unless the man invites you in. Don't take a roasting ear or melon unless he tells you to. If his dog barks at you, get away from it. Don't shoot it. Let them know we're their friends sent down to help them.

"As for the others: Place under arrest and bring into camp everybody else. Horseback or afoot, singly or in groups. Arrest them, fetch them into camp.

"Until further orders, all prisoners will be put under the old Spanish law—*la ley de fuga*—which means the prisoner is to be killed on the spot if a rescue is attempted."

The Nueces Strip that McNelly was charged with taming was as alive with bad characters as a rotting carcass is with maggots. He estimated that outlaws—some American, some Mexican—had killed more than two thousand ranchers and stolen nearly a million head of livestock, yet not one person had been tried and convicted in a court of law. No judge or jury dared; they would have paid almost instantly with their lives. McNelly determined to fight fire with fire, and the Constitution be damned.

"Those Nueces outlaws didn't fight by any books," Durham explained. "Neither did Captain McNelly. They made their own rules, and Captain made his. They didn't mind killing. Neither did Captain McNelly. They didn't take prisoners. Neither did Captain McNelly.

"I want to put this down to answer those people who have called Captain mean things all these years. With nothing but a commission from the governor, and without a dime of cash or even supplies, he was sent in to do a job that all others had failed to do and that had to be done if that Nueces Strip was ever to be livable for law-abiding folks."

No doubt some law-abiding folks fell victim to ranger six-gun justice along with the outlaws. The rangers were instructed to shoot first and not bother to ask questions later. Outlaws took a number of fancy saddles in a raid on Corpus Christi in March 1875, and McNelly told his men what to do if they spotted a rider in one of them: "Empty those saddles on sight. No palavering with the riders. Empty them. Leave the men where you drop them, and bring the saddles to camp." The consequences of the order can be inferred from the fact that while eighteen saddles were stolen, twenty-six were "emptied" and returned.

McNelly's Rangers used methods questioned by many, but their dedication and honor were beyond question. Pay was low—about $30 a month—and each ranger was required to furnish his own gun, horse, clothing, and other equipment. The state of Texas was supposed to supply food and ammunition, but often McNelly depended on merchants' taking his IOU. Grateful ranchers such as Richard King donated horses and rifles. Still, the rangers often went hungry, sometimes chewing mesquite beans to ease their pangs. Durham wore the farm boy clothes he enlisted in until they were in such bad shape he hid from women.

Outlaws in the Nueces Strip came in all colors, predominantly white and brown. Anglo outlaws such as King Fisher —whom we'll meet, with others of his kind, in a later chapter of this book—controlled the local law and the courts. When arrested, they were out on bail in no time. Mexican outlaws had the protection of the river. If they could get past the rangers and make it across the Rio Grande, they were home free.

Stealing Texas cattle and taking them back to Mexico was the major industry along the Rio Grande. The Mexicans, their national pride still smarting from defeats in 1836 and 1848, regarded cattle thieving as an honorable profession. McNelly determined to put a stop to it, and in the process came near starting another war with Mexico. In fact, that seems to have been his aim. A war would bring the United States military down on the area and put an end to the banditry.

Brazen thieves from the rancho at Las Cuevas, across the river from Rio Grande City, provided McNelly with the excuse he was looking for. Several hundred head of cattle were stolen in Texas and driven across the river to Las Cuevas, a stronghold commanded by General Juan Flores that served as headquarters for the thieves. McNelly arranged for covering fire from American troops in the area and boldly attacked with thirty rangers against at least ten times that many

Mexicans. General Flores was killed in the attack. The rangers were forced to fall back to the river and take cover under its bank. Although they were holding their own, McNelly appealed for help to the American troops, and about forty joined the rangers in Mexico, fighting off Mexicans trying to dislodge them.

American commanders recalled their troops to the American side, but NcNelly vowed not to leave Mexico until the stolen cattle were returned. His blood was up; facing hundreds of Mexican soldiers and civilians with only thirty men, he served notice on the Mexicans that he would give them an hour's notice before he recommenced his attack!

The next morning McNelley telegraphed a report to Austin and asked for instructions. The army, meantime, was keeping the wires to Washington hot. Washington, to say the least, was appalled at the prospect of being drawn into a war over a few cows. The State Department arranged with Mexican authorities for McNelly to surrender, but he replied that he "couldn't see it." At four o'clock in the afternoon, knowing he was on his own and keeping his word of giving an hour's notice before he moved, he sent the Mexicans notice to surrender the cattle or he would come and get them.

The Mexicans promptly agreed to deliver the cattle at ten o'clock the next morning, and McNelly at last withdrew to the Texas side of the river. The next day the Mexican in charge wrote McNelly a note saying that he was too busy to attend to the matter. McNelly sent a note right back in which he told an outrageous lie: that the American army was "awaiting your action in this matter." The Mexican found himself suddenly not busy at all, and the cattle were dispatched to the river.

Still playing games, the Mexican in charge of the herd of cattle stopped on the Mexican side of the river. Accounts differ as to what happened next. Ranger Bill Callicott later recalled the Mexican leader saying the cattle could not be crossed until they were inspected. McNelly pointed out the cattle had been crossed without being inspected when they were stolen, and he expected they could be recrossed the same way. At a signal from McNelly the rangers pulled their guns, and the Mexicans put the cattle across the river without further delay.

Ranger George Durham told a more colorful story. "When the ferry pulled up on the Mexican bank, Captain jumped over onto land, snubbed the boat for the old man, then dusted off his hands and looked up at the customs officers.

Catching criminals in the Nueces Strip required Texas Rangers to live outdoors for months at a time, poorly supplied and sometimes wearing clothes so ragged they would hide from women.

Texas Department of Public Safety

"There were five of them—a captain and four hands.

"...Captain was all polite. He shook the customs man by the hand and [said] ...we had come to take delivery of the cattle, and would he have his boys herd them down and cross them.

"This customs captain was also mighty polite. He explained that he had forgot this was Sunday. It was against their religion, he said, to do business on Sunday. In the morning, he promised. Early tomorrow morning they would deliver the herd. He was so sorry....

"We were expecting something, but it happened almost before we could lift our pistols. They drew.

"Captain McNelly was on top of that customs man like a cat, his pistol crashing the side of his head and his knee in the man's belly as he went down.

"We Rangers had a split-second advantage, I reckon. Our pistols cleared first. We had just automatically taken a skirmish position behind Captain...Bob Pitts shot the first one to clear leather before the man could bring his pistol up to firing level...and the fellow dropped like a polled shoat. The others dropped their pistols and reached....

"Captain had only stunned their head man and kicked out his breath. The man rolled over against his dead comrade and jerked back, stumbling to his feet. He was a plumb scared hombre. Captain grabbed him by the collar and hauled him up straight.

"Captain ordered McGovern, "Tell this man we're going to cross him over to the Texas bank, and for him to order his hands to deliver the cattle over in an hour or he dies. Tell him also if any rescue is tried he dies. Tell him."

"...It wasn't long till the cattle were started down to the river. Nobody was trying any monkey business."

The effect of this raid was salutary, on both sides of the river. Thirty-some-odd of the cattle wore Captain Richard King's Running W, and several rangers were detailed to deliver the cattle to him. King was astounded at their story of adventure.

"That was a daring trip," said Captain King. "There is not another man in the world who could invade a foreign country with that number of men and all get back alive. Captain McNelly is the first man that ever got stolen cattle out of Mexico. Out of thousands of head I have had stolen these are the only ones I ever got back, and I think more of them than of any five hundred head I have." King then had one horn sawed off each of the beeves and turned them loose with instructions to his ranch hands to let them wander unmolested the rest of their days. Those cattle had paid their dues; they were now retired.

Texas Rangers have come in for a great deal of criticism for the methods they used during these times, and indeed they broke many laws in the course of carrying out their duties. Without apologizing for their conduct, it must be pointed out that people who lived along the border—on both sides—could not or would not correct the situation themselves. In fairness to the rangers it must also be noted that what they did was not done for personal gain. The protestations of those whose rights were violated by the rangers must be heard against the backdrop of illegal activity in which they were engaged—or tolerating—and which the rangers were stopping.

Laredo stands for any number of towns made safe by the Texas Rangers. The dying cowboy in "Streets of Laredo" is Everyman of the border, a symbol of a way of life that could not be allowed to endure. Ironically, at the same time the Texas Rangers put an end to a violent era, they gave rise to some of its legendary characters and events.

Life was no more black and white on the streets of Laredo in those times than it is today.

By the 1890s the Texas Rangers had pacified the frontier and gone on to assignments symbolic of an era of change: This group restored peace in Temple during a railroad strike in 1894.

Texas Department of Public Safety

4

Cynthia Ann Parker

FEW SITUATIONS IN HISTORY SEEM TO have aroused such mingled feelings of pity and disgust as the capture of white women by members of the group variously called Native Americans, First Americans, Indians, indigenous peoples, redskins, savages, and so on, depending on the speaker's bias. Such women, if recaptured, were often pitied because it was assumed they had been raped and, in effect, ruined. They were regarded as damaged goods that had somehow been rendered unfit for "polite" society. Ironically, the root of their suffering—which was very real—lay not in their treatment at the hands of their captors but in the prejudices of their liberators.

Many captives did suffer violent, degrading treatment at the hands of the Indians. Yet there are far too many instances of white captives who "went native" and thoroughly enjoyed the wild, free life of the Indian to suppose that captivity inevitably led to permanent psychological damage. (I will use the terms *Indian* and *Native American* interchangeably. Years of textbook writing has made me sensitive not only to the fact that various minority groups prefer to be called one thing or another, but also to the fact that from time to time they change their minds about how they want to be identified. Since this is not a textbook and I don't have to worry about such things, I won't, except to avoid the use of deliberately prejudicial labels. The general public is familiar with both the terms above.)

Whites who preferred life with the Indians to being returned to their homes and families presented a puzzlement to people of the time. The reason is easy to discern. Indians were the enemy, and most people subscribed to the theory that the only good Indian was a dead one. Racial prejudice no doubt also played a part. People whose only experience with

Indians was painted warriors killing friends or family naturally had quite a different view of them than did people who lived with them for a long period. Obviously, there had to be another side to Indians besides the violent one they showed in battle, but admitting so would have been difficult in frontier times, especially in front of people whose families or friends had been killed, often in gruesome fashion. (Indians no doubt felt the same about whites.)

The real tragedy of Cynthia Ann Parker was not that she was captured by Indians but that, once recaptured, well-meaning family members she no longer knew or loved prevented her from returning to the only home where she truly belonged.

* * * * *

Preloch - Cynthia Ann Parker

by Michael Stevens
arr. Stevens/Seyer

Cynthia Ann Parker

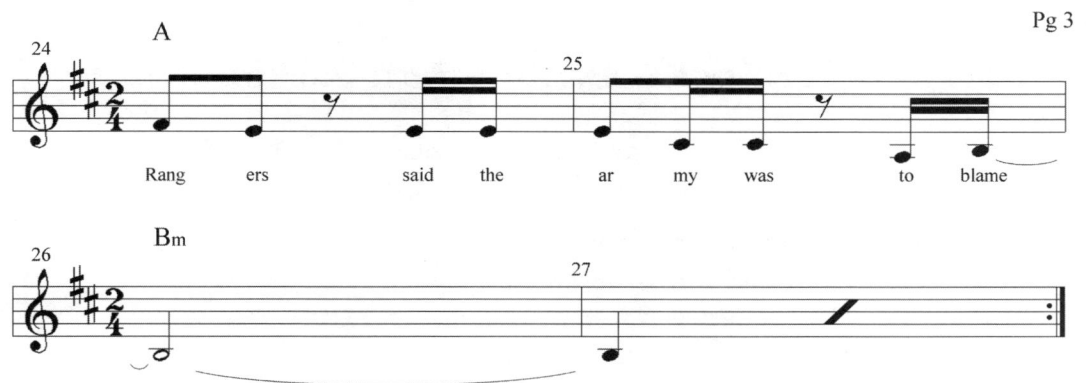

Rang ers said the ar my was to blame

Preloch – Cynthia Ann Parker

by Michael Stevens

Some twenty-four years since '36
When Comanches stole her away
The civilized world would reclaim her
On a horrible, death-filled day

Young Quanah was a witness
To what they called, the Pease River Fight
In truth, mostly women, massacred
By a horde of savage whites

Charlie Goodnight was a scout that day
He disputed Sul Ross's claim
But he praised the honor of the Rangers
Said the army was to blame

She stood straight and proud, said "me Cynthia Ann"
Smote hard upon her breast
These few words, we know for sure
Have to guess about the rest

They dragged her around and showed her off
Like a prize from a county fair
Dressed her up in ridiculous clothes
They wouldn't even wear

They only saw her rescued
Not ripped from family
With a deaf-ear turned, they ignored her tears
Only death would set her free

Now she rests in the ground, on a white man's fort
With a daughter and a loving son
Far from grief and misery
Her hell on earth is done

But their spirits soar, beyond the setting sun
In a world that has no dread
Where you never grow old, and there is no war
In the Comanche, Land of the Dead

The water is clear, and the days are warm
In the Comanche, Land of the Dead
The lodges are filled with happiness
The buffalo keeps them fed

Preloch watches her children play
Tends to the family stead
On the grassy plains, of eternity
In the Comanche, Land of the Dead

Puk saw, numa nai
Kay y nai

esearching the life of Cynthia Ann Parker was somewhat frustrating. While the subject has fascinated many writers, the plain truth is that most of them have written much and known little. None of her contemporaries seems to have done the one thing I would have wanted to do had I known her: Get her to tell her life story and put it in writing in her own words. Whether this was because people who knew her were so busy feeling sorry for Cynthia Ann Parker they took no time to ask her about her life, or because they failed to set down what she told them, or because she would not speak of her feelings about her life and its events, I do not know.

Unlike some others who have preceded me, however, I will not make up something.

At any rate, published accounts of Cynthia Ann Parker's life give a detailed account of her capture and, after that, wind up being mostly about other people in some way connected with her. By the time you finish reading a book supposedly about Cynthia Ann Parker, you know a great deal about almost everyone in the book except its main subject.

In the writing business, this is called padding. I hope not to be judged guilty of this crime.

For this reason, I will not attempt to go into all the gory details of Cynthia Ann Parker's capture, nor will I speculate on what could have happened while she lived with the Comanches, or repeat what other people think happened. That has all been done many times before. Instead, I will gracefully accept that there is a lot about Cynthia Ann Parker we do not know and never will. It is my belief that to attempt to fabricate a life history for her would be lousy history and show disrespect for her memory.

I *will* quote from various writings about Cynthia Ann Parker's life in order to illustrate how biased the traditional accounts of her life are. As with the things people say about you and me today, most likely the truth lies somewhere between the opinions of friends and enemies, or in her case, between the opinions of those who felt sorry for her because she had been carried away by Indians, and those Indians who loved her as a member of their family.

Cynthia Ann Parker

The bare bones of the Cynthia Ann Parker story are this: She and several others were taken captive on May 19, 1836, at Fort Parker, Texas, near present-day Mexia, when Cynthia Ann was nine years old. Some twenty-four years later, she and a daughter were captured and returned to her white family. After living with whites again for about ten years, she followed her daughter to the grave. One of her Indian sons, Quanah, became the last great war chief of the Comanches.

Almost everything else that has been written about Cynthia Ann Parker was based on conjecture or the observations of others, yet the romantic appeal of her story is such that numerous writers have felt compelled to do what she herself never did: Tell her story. A sampling of the results follows.

A number of Parkers were killed when Indians, probably Apaches, attacked Fort Parker. Cynthia Ann Parker was captured and later traded to Comanches, who became her new family.

The UT Institute of Texan Cultures at San Antonio, No. 75-566

Indian Depredations in Texas, by J. W. Wilbarger, was published in 1888. It was written at a time when memories of the war to take the Indians' lands were quite fresh. His account of Cynthia Ann Parker reflects the popular view of the time, that Indian captives—especially women—were only to be pitied. In telling of a group of traders who met with Cynthia Ann after she had been five years a captive, Wilbarger states, "She came and sat down by the root of a tree, and while their presence was doubtless a happy event to the poor stricken captive, who, in her doleful captivity, had endured everything but death, she refused to speak a word. As she sat there, musing, perhaps, of distant relatives and friends, and the bereavements at the beginning and progress of their distress, they employed every persuasive art to evoke some expression."

What Wilbarger was doing, of course, was attributing thoughts and feelings to Cynthia Ann he had no way of knowing were correct or not.

In telling of her life as the wife of the Indian chief Peta Nocona, Wilbarger continued freely using prejudicial adjectives to paint a picture of a life he knew nothing about. "Cynthia Ann . . . became the bride of Peta Nocona, performing for her imperious lord all the slavish offices which savageism and Indian custom assigns as the duty of a wife." He quotes another visitor to the Comanche camp who referred to the children of her marriage as "little, naked barbarians" and to her husband as a "great, greasy, lazy buck sleeping in the shade . . . whose first utterance upon arousing would be a stern command to his meek, pale faced wife."

All that may well have been true, but at least to some degree it could also have been said of a great many white families of the time. At any rate, the point is that the descriptions were based on what people *thought* or *wanted to believe* Cynthia Ann Parker felt or experienced.

Just how reliable the second-hand accounts of Cynthia Ann Parker's life were may be inferred from the story of her recapture at the Massacre of Pease River in December 1860. Sul Ross, a participant in the battle who built a reputation as a great Indian fighter on his account of the fight and used it to get himself elected governor of Texas, described the Massacre of Pease River as a great victory over a horde of fierce Comanche warriors. Ross further claimed to have killed Peta Nocona, Cynthia Ann Parker's husband, in this battle.

Wilbarger quotes Ross's account of the battle and rhapsodizes, "And thus was fought the battle of Pease river, between a superior force of Comanches under the implacable chief, Peta Nocona on one side, and sixty rangers led by their youthful commander, Captain L. S. Ross, on the other. Ross, sword in hand, led the furious rush of the rangers; and in the desperate encounter of 'war to the knife' which ensued, nearly all the warriors bit the dust."

The only problem with the story was, it was a bunch of lies.

Charles Goodnight, later to become a famous rancher, founder of the Goodnight-Loving Trail, and friend of Quanah Parker, flatly contradicted Ross' story and late in life fumed over his use of the story of a "great victory" to boost his political career. Goodnight was a scout at the Massacre of Pease River and described the behavior of the rangers and the soldiers with them in entirely different terms. "The rangers passed through the squaws and shot the bucks as they came to them. The Sergeant and his men fell in behind on the squaws, whose horses were loaded so heavily with buffalo meat, tent poles, and camp equipage that they could not run, and killed every one of them, almost in a pile."

In modern terms, a group of neighborhood women and a couple of carryout boys were killed in a supermarket parking lot while loading their purchases into minivans.

(I have been deliberately playing with your mind here. Have you ever noticed that whenever Indians killed even a few whites, the engagement was called a massacre, but when whites killed Indians— dozens or even hundreds—it was called a battle? History *is* written by the victors, and this is one of the little tricks writers have used for years to color their narratives. How did you feel when you read the word *massacre* applied to a fight in which whites slaughtered Indians?)

Those who took part in the fight later claimed to have engaged as many as six hundred Comanches, including two hundred well-armed warriors. However, Indian descendants of Cynthia Ann Parker tell a different story, one that is confirmed by other participants in the fight.

Ross and his force had stumbled onto the camp of a hunting party after all the warriors had left. The people in the camp were Mexican slaves and Indian women left behind to pack up all the meat and carry it back to the main camp. "I was in the Pease River fight," one man later said, "but I am not very proud of it. That was not a battle at all, but just a killing of squaws. One or two bucks and sixteen squaws were killed." Goodnight expressed shame at the conduct of the soldiers. "To the credit of the old Texas Rangers, not one of them shot a squaw that day. The Sergeant in charge of the military squad probably did not know them from bucks and probably did not care." As for Ross' claim to have killed Chief Peta Nocona, the fact seems to be that the dead man was Nocona's personal servant, a Mexican named Joe. Comanche descendants of Quanah Parker later stated that Nocona was away from the camp at the time of the attack. Quanah —a teenager at the time of the attack— was old enough to be a reliable witness, and family history is that Nocona returned after the battle and gathered up the hidden survivors scattered over the prairie, including Quanah.

Misery plainly shows on Cynthia Ann Parker's face in this photograph of her and Prairie Flower (Toh-tsee-ah) taken after their return to their white family.

George Barnard Papers, The Texas Collection, Baylor University, Waco, Texas

One fact not in dispute is that two members of the Indian party were captured during the action while trying to escape. Tom Kelliher chased a mounted Indian some distance. He was about to shoot the rider when he discovered it was a woman carrying an infant. The woman held up the baby, he said, and cried out that she was an American. It was Cynthia Ann Parker and her daughter, Toh-tsee-ah (Prairie Flower, given as Topsannah in some accounts. The name Toh-tsee-ah appears on her tombstone at Fort Sill, Oklahoma.).

"The squaw was in terrible grief," Goodnight said. "Through sympathy for her, thinking her distress would be the same as that of our women under similar circumstances, I thought I would try to console her and make her understand that she would not be hurt. When I got near her I noticed that she had blue eyes and light hair, which had been cut short. It was a little difficult to distinguish her blond features, as her face and hands were extremely dirty from handling so much meat.

"...Her grief was distressing and intense, and I shall never forget the impression it made on me."

Cynthia Ann was grieving because her two sons, Quanah and Pecos, were missing after the battle, and she feared they were both dead.

While her captors were familiar with the story of her capture and suspected the identity of their prisoner, it was not until she was questioned by her uncle, Isaac Parker, days later that she responded dramatically to the mention of her name. Rising, she smote her breast and said forcefully, "Me, Cynthia Ann." Questioned further, she described Fort Parker and her capture and recalled that she had once had palefaced parents.

Isaac Parker took Toh-tsee-ah and Cynthia Ann, or Preloch, as she was known to her Comanche family, home with him to Birdville, in Tarrant County, stopping in Fort Worth to have them photographed together. Her well-meaning white relatives, unable to accept the fact that she preferred her Indian family and life, immediately started trying to eradicate all traces of the major part of her existence while she continued to grieve for the loss of her two sons. Foiled in her attempts to escape and search for her family in the wilderness, she sat on the Parkers' front porch for hours at a time, clutching Topsannah to her breast, tears streaming down her face.

Whites vacillated between feelings of pity because of Cynthia Ann's supposed "long night of suffering and woe"—speculated about in numerous newspaper stories—and the same repulsed fascination and titillation that attract people to carnival sideshows. The womenfolk of the community outfitted Cynthia Ann in clothing that even white women of the time found uncomfortable and paraded her before the Secession Convention in Austin in early 1861. While the white

Cynthia Ann Parker's oldest child, Quanah, became the last great war chief of the Comanches. Later in life he led efforts to reconcile the Indians to reservation life.

The UT Institute of Texan Cultures at San Antonio, No. 89-121

women enjoyed being the center of attention as caretakers of the biggest sideshow freak to hit town in years, Cynthia Ann became convinced the delegates had been assembled to decide her fate. Terrified, she tried to run away once more.

After a time Cynthia Ann and Prairie Flower went to live with Orlena and Ruff O'Quinn, her sister and brother-in-law. Neighbors cutely began calling Toh-tsee-ah "Tecks Ann" and took her visiting to show her off. Toh-tsee-ah contracted influenza and died at the age of five in December 1863. Heartbroken and now without any member of the family she loved, Cynthia Ann herself died of the flu in 1870.

Following his surrender in 1875, Quanah Parker immediately began seeking information of his mother. Learning of her death, he began efforts to have her remains moved to Cache, Oklahoma, his home. This was done in 1910, and at the reburial Quanah spoke lovingly of his mother and said she never wanted to leave her Comanche family and return to the whites. Quanah took his place beside her just three months later. In 1957 both were removed to the military cemetery at Fort Sill, Oklahoma, and in 1965 Toh-tsee-ah joined them.

Cynthia Ann Parker's Indian descendants, handing down family stories, insist that she was happy with her life as a Comanche. Whether this was so we cannot tell. The record is clear that her life with her white kin was desperately unhappy after her return. The reasons for this we can only guess at.

Cynthia Ann Parker suffered a dual tragedy and died in misery. Happy as a young child, she was ripped from the white world and flung headlong into an alien one. Twenty-four years later she suffered another transition as abrupt and shocking. Now she belonged to neither the world of the Comanches nor the world of the whites.

Comanches believed that after death their spirits journeyed to the land of the dead, beyond the setting sun. This land was like the one left behind, except that all bad things about that world were no more. Everybody in the land of the dead was young. There they and their loved ones dwelt in a place where there was no war, no darkness, no sorrow.

May Cynthia Ann Parker dwell in the Comanche land of the dead forever and ever.

❦ 5 ❧

The Battle of Adobe Walls

THE BATTLE OF ADOBE WALLS, ONE OF the most famous and exciting Indian battles ever to take place in Texas, must be seen in a larger context. A number of forces were in motion that just happened to come together at a tiny outpost on the Canadian River. Those forces all brought a crushing weight to bear on one common point: the Plains Indians.

Politicians and bureaucrats of the 1870s had not yet learned to equivocate and obfuscate with the consummate skill of their modern counterparts. They tended to say what they meant. The Commissioner of Indian Affairs had this to say about the Indians in his report of 1872, two years before the Battle of Adobe Walls. "No one will rejoice more heartily than the present Commissioner when the Indians of this country cease to be in a position to dictate, in any form or degree, to the Government; when, in fact, the last hostile tribe becomes reduced to the condition of suppliants for charity. This is, indeed, the only hope of salvation for the aborigines of the continent. If they stand up against the progress of civilization and industry, they must be relentlessly crushed. The westward course of population is neither to be denied nor delayed for the sake of all the Indians that ever called this country their home. They must yield or perish; and there is something that savors of providential mercy in the rapidity with which their fate advances upon them...."

There is a tendency to forget that the Indians knew they were engaged in a battle for survival not only of their physical being but also of their entire way of life. For this reason they fought with the fury born of desperation. For the whites the struggle was a matter of control of the land—"the westward course of population is neither to be denied nor delayed."

The key to white success was destruction of the Indians, but that was, even in 1872, not politically popular, as the Commissioner noted. "...The government has seemed somewhat tardy...in applying the scourge to individuals and bands leaving their prescribed limits [the reservation] without authority, or for hostile purposes. This has been partly from a *legitimate deference* [emphasis added] to the conviction of the great body of citizens [i.e., a majority of the people of the United States] that the Indians have been in the past unjustly and cruelly treated, and that great patience and long forbearance ought to be exercised in bringing them around to submission...."

Let me translate the Commissioner's remarks: The Constitution of the United States provides that the government shall

Nearly everything you see in this Plains Indian camp came from the buffalo, from shields to tepees to clothes to the bone scraper the woman is using to remove the meat from a buffalo hide.

The UT Institute of Texan Cultures at San Antonio, No. 74-687

carry out the will of the people, and the great majority of Americans wanted the Indians to be treated fairly. Square that, if you can, with the remarks quoted earlier that the Indians must be "relentlessly crushed," must "yield or perish."

Obviously, the government had a problem. It wanted to kill or subdue the Indians, but the public was not in favor of how it wanted to go about the job. Now, what does our government do today when it can't openly do its own dirty work because that might cost politicians votes? It gets someone else to do it while it turns a blind eye. That much has *not* changed in the last century.

Enter the buffalo hunters, who had the incentive—$3 per hide—to wipe out the one thing that supported the entire Plains Indian culture, providing them food, clothing, and shelter. Take away the buffalo, the Indians' livelihood, and they would be forced to accept reservation life. That was common knowledge.

General Philip Sheridan prophesied to the Texas Legislature, urging them not to pass a law for the protection of the buffalo. "These men [the hide hunters] have done in the last two years, and will do in the next year, more to settle the vexed Indian question than the entire regular Army has done in the last thirty years. They are destroying the Indians' commissary; and it is a well known fact that an army losing its base of supplies is placed at a great disadvantage. Send them powder and lead, if you will; but, for the sake of lasting peace, let them kill, skin, and sell until the buffaloes are exterminated. Then your prairies can be covered with speckled cattle and the festive cowboy, who follows the hunter as a second forerunner of an advanced civilization."

The Battle of Adobe Walls was not the beginning of the end for the Plains Indians. That had happened long before—on October 12, 1492, to be exact, when the first European set foot in the Americas and said, in effect, "To hell with all you people who've lived here for centuries, this place is *mine.*" Instead, the battle was one more link in a chain of events that dispossessed America's native peoples.

* * * * *

The Battle of Adobe Walls

by Michael Stevens

The sun and stars, they do not change
And the seasons move on and on
The Indian knew the old ways would not
If the buffalo herds were gone

The Indian did not understand
The white man's words and deeds
This man with spotted buffalo
Who kills more than he needs

Read the words of Ten Bears
Black Elk, and Plenty Coup
They, like many, knew their way of life
And the land they loved, they could lose

So they met where Elk Creek meets
The northern fork of the Red River
Forced to stand, make their final plea
A message death would have to deliver

Perhaps this helps explain Adobe Walls
The "why" of what the Indians had done
Though, in the end, when the horses died
The white man finally won

They had not set out to subdue the savages
Barely considered them as people living there
They sought adventure and money, three dollars a hide
Unconcerned at being fair

So they built their post called Adobe Walls
On the range of the last buffalo
Vowed not to fight if they were left alone
They'd just take and take and then go

The attack came at sunrise
Out of the blazing dawn
Like a pretty wave of coals from a campfire shovel
That flowed around them, on and on

They held for three days, with little loss of life
Bullets and arrows thumped the sod halls
The hunters, outnumbered I reckon, forty to one
No Indian victory was claimed at Adobe Walls

Two monuments, side by side, at Adobe Walls
Honor, passion, and what it makes man do
One for the Indians, they loved their land
One for Dixon, he loved it, too

About now all the descendants of people who had family members killed by Indians are probably busily organizing a lynch party to find me and dispense a little frontier justice in my direction. You needn't bother.

The awful tragedy—or the simple truth, depending on how you want to look at it—of the defeat of the Indians is that there is simply no way it could have been avoided, given the circumstances of the times. It is easy for us to sit safely at a computer keyboard and moralize now, but had we been living on the Texas frontier in the 1800s and been attacked by Indians, we would have fought back. If Indians had killed members of my family, I would have been out there trying to kill Indians, too. By the same token, if I had been an Indian, I would have been killing whites to try to save my way of life.

History can be rewritten, but what happened can't be changed, so it is pointless at this time to do too much breast-beating and bemoaning of the fate of the Indians. Any student of the past knows that if history shows anything, it is that any time there is a weaker people, a stronger one will eventually overrun it. How long it takes for that to happen depends to a great extent on how valuable the land and resources of the weaker people happen to be. America is a rich land, and it would be well for those of us who are the current inhabitants of this continent to remember the lessons of the past. Someday it may be our turn.

Many people fall into the trap of trying to assign blame to the whites or to the Indians. Some say the Indians were murdering savages and the whites were justified in using any means to eradicate them. Others say the whites lied to the Indians, stole from them, broke treaty after treaty with them, killed Indians indiscriminately, and never gave the Indians a chance to live peacefully with them.

There is a lot of evidence to support both arguments, and trying to resolve the whole dispute now in favor of one side or the other would be as productive as trying to regain one's virginity. What's done is done, and about all we can do is go forward from where we are now.

Which way is forward? Unfortunately, only history will tell. We're in the same trap life sprang on the Indians: Events beyond our personal control are rapidly changing our world. So read carefully the words of Michael Stevens' poem about the Battle of Adobe Walls. He may be speaking about another place and time, but in many ways, he could also be talking about you.

The Battle of Adobe Walls

Perhaps 40 million buffalo roamed the Great Plains at the peak of their era. Flowing back and forth across the land, they provided a limitless, though seasonal, food supply for the Indians. The Indians eagerly awaited the coming of the annual migrations, for it meant a time of plenty and the chance to lay by stores of food for use after the buffalo moved on. Once the Indians got the horse, however, they could follow the buffalo herds. Now able to get all the food they needed year round, their culture bloomed.

Buffalo became the center of the Plains Indians' way of life in a way that went far beyond what a job means to modern peoples. W. W. Newcomb said, "Seldom has any other animal provided so many basic cultural requirements. In one way or another, buffaloes provided food, both for immediate and future use, shelter, clothing, weapons, tools of various sorts, bedding, ropes, glue, cosmetics, fuel, and drink. It is almost unnecessary to remark that when the 'inexhaustible' herds of buffalo became extinct, the cultures which had come to lean so completely on them collapsed."

And don't think for a minute the Indians did not see what was happening to them and what the final outcome would be when whites began taking their lands and killing the buffalo. Hear their words.

"By the time I was forty, I could see our country was changing fast, and that these changes were causing us to live very differently. Anybody could now see that soon there would be no buffalo on the plains and everybody was wondering how we could live after they were gone . . . . White men with their spotted-buffalo [cattle] were on the plains about us. Their houses were near the water-holes, and their villages on the rivers. We made up our minds to be friendly with them, in spite of all the changes they were bringing. But we found this difficult, because the white men too often promised to do one thing and then when they acted at all, did another.

"They spoke very loudly when they said their laws were made for everybody; but we soon learned that although they expected us to keep them, they thought nothing of breaking them themselves. They told us not to drink whisky, yet they made it themselves and traded it to us for furs and robes until both were nearly gone. Their Wise Ones said we might have their religion, but when we tried to understand it we found that there were too many kinds of religion among white men for us to understand, and that scarcely any two white men agreed which was the right one to learn. This bothered us a good deal until we saw that the white man did not take his religion any more seriously than he did his laws, and that he kept both of them just behind him, like Helpers, to use when they might do him good in his dealings with strangers. These were not our ways. We kept the laws we made and lived our religion. We have never been able to understand the white man, who fools nobody but himself."

—Aleek-chea-ahoosh (Plenty-Coups), Crow chief

"I had never seen a Wasichu [white man] then, and did not know what one looked like; but everyone was saying that the Wasichus were coming and that they were going to take our country and rub us all out and that we should all have to die fighting.

"Once we were happy in our own country and we were seldom hungry, for then the two-leggeds and the four-leggeds lived together like relatives, and there was plenty for them and for us. But the Wasichus came, and they have made little islands for us and other little islands for the four-leggeds, and always these islands are becoming smaller, for around them surges the gnawing flood of the Wasichu; and it is dirty with lies and greed.

"... I can remember when the bison were so many that they could not be counted, but more and more Wasichus came to kill them until there were only heaps of bones scattered where they used to be. The Wasichus did not kill them to eat; they killed them for the metal that makes them crazy, and they took only the hides to sell. Sometimes they did not even take the hides, only the tongues; and I have heard that fire-boats came down the Missouri River loaded with dried bison tongues. You can see that the men who did this were crazy. Sometimes they did not even take the tongues; they just killed and killed because they liked to do that. When we hunted bison, we killed only what we needed."

—Hehaka Sapa (Black Elk), Sioux chief

"In the old times we were strong. We used to hunt and fish. We raised our little crop of corn and melons and ate the mesquite beans. Now all is changed. We eat the white man's food, and it makes us soft; we wear the white man's heavy clothing and it makes us weak. Each day in the old times in summer and in winter we came down to the riverbanks to bathe. This strengthened and toughened our firm skin. But white settlers were shocked to see the naked Indians, so now we keep away. In old days we wore the breechcloth, and aprons made of bark and reeds. We worked all winter in the wind—bare arms, bare legs, and never felt the cold. But now, when the wind blows down from the mountains it makes us cough. Yes—we know that when you come, *we die.*

—Chiparopai, Yuma woman

"My people have never first drawn a bow or fired a gun against the whites. There has been trouble on the line between us, and my young men have danced the war dance. But it was not begun by us. It was you who sent the first soldier and we who sent out the second. Two years ago I came upon this road, following the buffalo, that my wives and children might have their cheeks plump and their bodies warm. But the soldiers fired on us, and since that time, there has been a noise like that of a thunderstorm, and we have not known which way to go. . . .

Buffalo hunters were interested only in the profits they could make from hides and tongues; unregulated hunting came near to totally eradicating the estimated 60 million buffalo that once roamed North America.

The UT Institute of Texan Cultures at San Antonio, No. 74-948

"Nor have we been made to cry once alone. The blue dressed soldiers...came from out of the night when it was dark and still, and for campfires they lit our lodges. Instead of hunting game they killed my braves, and the warriors of the tribe cut their hair for the dead. So it was in Texas. They made sorrow come into our camps, and we went out like the buffalo bulls when their cows are attacked. When we found them, we killed them and their scalps hung in our lodges.

"The Comanches are not weak and blind, like the pups of the dog when seven sleeps old. They are strong and far-sighted, like grown horses. We took their road and we went on it. The white women cried and our women laughed.

"...If the Texans had kept out of my country there might have been peace. But that which you now say we must live on is too small. The Texans have taken away the places where the grass grew the thickest and the timber was the best. Had we kept that, we might have done the things you ask. But it is too late. The white man has the country which we loved, and we only wish to wander on the prairies until we die."

—Parra-Wa-Samen (Ten Bears), Comanche chief

Ironically, the chief who led the Comanches in their last stand against the whites killing the buffalo was himself half white. He was Quanah, son of Cynthia Ann Parker and Peta Nocona. The final struggle began at a smudge on the map in the Texas Panhandle called Adobe Walls.

The slaughter of the buffalo had been going on at a headlong pace for years. By the early 1870s buffalo hunters noticed that the huge herds had virtually disappeared from the northern Great Plains. Some felt there were two herds, northern and southern, and that the northern herd had simply been shot out; others theorized that buffalo feared to cross the new transcontinental railroad and remained south of it. Whatever the reason, in the 1870s buffalo hunters turned their attention to the last stronghold of the buffalo, the Texas Panhandle. Coincidentally, this also happened to be the last stronghold of the Comanches and other tribes who had refused to go onto the reservations.

Typical of its dealings with the Indians, the United States government, in the Medicine Lodge Treaty of 1867, overreached itself when it promised the Indians it would keep buffalo hunters from ranging south of the Arkansas River. There was no way the army could seal the hundreds of miles of border between the Indian hunting grounds and the whites. In addition, most of the land lay in Texas, which had retained its public lands when it joined the Union, and the federal government had no authority to ban anyone from the territory. Such subtleties were lost on the Indians, who felt they had been guaranteed sole access to the area. The Indians felt betrayed once again when buffalo hunters began showing up in territory they had been promised for the umpty-leventh time was reserved for them.

Established in 1874 on the Canadian River twenty miles northeast of present-day Borger to supply buffalo hunters, the trading post of Adobe Walls symbolized the threat to the Indians' existence. William Bent had operated an earlier post by the same name a mile or so away in the 1840s, but the purpose of that post had been to buy horses the Comanches stole in Mexico and did not attract their ire. The new Adobe Walls was an entirely different matter.

Aggravating the situation was the fact that by 1874 many tribes had been forced onto reservations in Indian Territory (now Oklahoma), where they had the opportunity to observe firsthand on a daily basis the wickedness and inventiveness whites were capable of when it came to cheating the Indians. Government contractors routinely supplied the Indians with shoddy clothes and shorted them on rations, stealing from both the government and the Indians with impunity. Hungry Indians could almost see the buffalo herds in the Texas Panhandle from the camps where they were starving, and no amount of white man's logic could convince them they should not leave the reservation and bring back buffalo meat to feed their families.

The Indians realized they had one last chance to save the buffalo and themselves, and that was to throw the buffalo hunters out of the Texas Panhandle. Attacks were made on isolated buffalo hunters' camps in the spring of 1874, but the Indians knew that concerted action was needed. In June the Southern Plains tribes called a meeting—off the reservation—just north of present-day Altus, Oklahoma, where Elk Creek meets the North Fork of the Red River. The purpose: Develop a plan to stop the whites' destruction of the last of the buffalo.

Stone Calf led the Cheyennes, Lone Wolf the Kiowas, Quanah Parker the Comanches. Quanah had just assumed the role of war chief at a Sun Dance in late May, replacing the mortally ill Bull Bear. Each chief spoke, stating his people's grievances against the whites. But the star of the council was a young Comanche medicine man, Isatai (Coyote Droppings).

Isatai's stock had risen a year earlier, when he accurately predicted that a comet would disappear in five days and be followed by a drought. Desperate for hope, the assembled tribes listened as Isatai told of his recent ascent above the clouds to speak directly with the Great Spirit. The Great Spirit, Isatai said, had told him how to make a paint that would turn bullets. The Great Spirit had also given him a message for the chiefs: They should not make peace with the whites, and if they killed the white hunters, the buffalo would come back everywhere. Isatai proposed that the first attack be on the buffalo hunters at Adobe Walls.

At the time of the attack, Adobe Walls was but a few months old. Buyers of buffalo hides at Dodge City, Kansas, saw in 1873 that the supply was dwindling. During the latter part of that year buffalo hunter and scout Billy Dixon and some companions made a wide circle down into the forbidden territory of the Texas Panhandle, and what they saw convinced them plenty of hides remained to be taken there. In March 1874 Dixon went to Dodge City and began talking up the Panhandle. A. C. Meyers, a merchant in Dodge, proposed that any hunter who wanted to go should load up his wagons with supplies, and Meyers would pay him to freight them to Adobe Walls, where he would then sell the supplies to the hunters at Dodge City prices.

People flocked to join the expedition, including James Hanrahan, a big-time buffalo hunter, and Bat Masterson, a youngster just starting to forge a reputation and career that would span much of the West. The trip to Adobe Walls was one big party. "There was never a happier lot of men in the world," Dixon later recalled. "All were in rugged health, none in need, most of them inured to the hardships of life in the wilderness, each confident that he could take care of himself, sure of the help of his comrades in any emergency, and everybody as merry and jolly as could be. If there was care of any kind, it was too light to be felt. We ate like wolves, and could have digested a dry buffalo hide with the hair on. Spring was on the way, and the air was light and buoyant, making the days and nights an endless delight.

"...Best of all, when we camped at night, there would be singing, dancing, music and telling tales. In the party were a number of veterans of the Civil War, with endless stories of desperate battles that were greatly to our liking."

Soon the revelers would be engaged in a desperate battle of their own that would not be so much to their liking. Yet they pushed on, after a brief meeting on the banks of the Cimarron in which they agreed that, if they met Indians, they would be friendly if the Indians were. In that peculiar logic that lets humans see things as they want to see them and not as they are (thus explaining political parties), the buffalo hunters invading Indian territory they knew was off limits decided, said Dixon, "This was their country...and if they would leave us alone, we would be willing to leave them alone." How generous of them.

Soon the caravan reached a broad valley near a stream called East Adobe Walls Creek, and there they decided to make permanent camp. All fell to work, Dixon said. "Myers and Leonard built a picket house twenty by sixty feet in size. James Hanrahan put up a sod house, twenty-five by sixty, in which he opened a saloon. Thomas O'Keefe built a blacksmith's shop of pickets, fifteen feet square. Thus, a little town was sprouting in the wilderness —a place where we could buy something to eat and wear, something to drink, ammunition for our guns, and a place where our wagons, so necessary in expeditions like ours, could be repaired.

"While all this hammering and pounding and digging was going on, I started with three companions and rode the country as far down as where the present town of Clarendon, Texas, now stands. We were absent about fifteen days, and upon our return we found the buildings about finished. . . .

"During our absence from camp, Rath & Wright came down from Dodge City with another outfit and built a sod house sixteen by twenty feet. This firm bought buffalo hides and was engaged in general merchandising."

Shortly, buffalo began arriving in the area from farther south, and the killing began. "Where buffalo were as plentiful as they were here I could easily kill enough in a day to keep ten skinners busily at work," Dixon said. ". . . This was deadly business, without sentiment; it was dollars against tenderheartedness, and dollars won."

Indians coursed the area, too, and attacked buffalo hunters' camps. Adobe Walls was "buzzing" with talk of Indians. They knew full well the reason for the Indian attacks, Dixon said. "All of us felt that these murders had been perpetrated as a warning to the buffalo-hunters to leave the country...

"Every man of us was dead set against abandoning the buffalo range. The herds were now at hand, and we were in a fair way to make big money. Furthermore, the buffalo were becoming scarcer and scarcer each year, and it was expedient that we make hay while the sun shone, for soon the sun would be no longer shining in the buffalo business. Its night was close at hand."

In late June Dixon went into Adobe Walls to stock up on supplies for the remainder of the summer. By June 26 his wagons were loaded and ready to pull out the next morning. A little niggling worry kept eating at Dixon, making him uneasy; he later said, "There was Indian in the air. . . ." Little did he know just how much Indian was in the air around Adobe Walls.

Meanwhile, the night before returning to the buffalo range was a good time for a party. Hanrahan's saloon offered the best venue between Dodge City and Santa Fe, and the rowdy buffalo hunters went at it. Twenty-eight men and one woman happened to be present. As the party wound down, first one and then another spread his blankets on the ground outside, tucking his rifle at his side, between the blankets, to protect it from dew or rain. Some bedded down on Hanrahan's saloon floor. Every door to every building stood wide open, and a marvelous Panhandle night descended. "Those were splendid nights, out there under the stars. The mornings came with dazzling splendor. At this season sunrise on the Plains presented a scene of magnificence. I always had the feeling that it came with a thunderous sound," Dixon said.

The morning of June 27 was to arrive with more than just a thunderous sound. Only a few miles away camped nearly a thousand Indian warriors, who planned to howl up the sun as they swooped down on Adobe Walls.

Billy Dixon was not the only person to sense impending danger. James Hanrahan had been warned by the white husband of an Indian woman that an attack would come at dawn, catching the sleeping hunters in their beds. About two o'clock in the morning, a crack like that of a rifle shot awakened the camp. Hanrahan shouted for those sleeping in his saloon to get out; the ridgepole that supported the sod roof was breaking, he said. Actually, as was discovered years later, Hanrahan had fired a shot to awaken them.

Everyone pitched in to support the supposedly sagging roof. While some fashioned a prop from a forked log found on the woodpile, others climbed to the roof and removed some of the sod. Continuing his subterfuge, Hanrahan fussed over the repairs until the eastern sky had begun to gray, then set up drinks on the house as the sky grew red.

It was now too late to go back to bed, so Dixon went outside to roll up his blankets and stow them in the wagon. "As I turned to pick up my gun, which lay on the ground, I looked in the direction of our horses," he said. "They were in sight. Something else caught my eye. Just beyond the horses, at the edge of some timber, was a large body of objects advancing vaguely in the dusky dawn toward our stock and in the direction of Adobe Walls. Though keen of vision, I could not make out what the objects were, even by straining my eyes.

"Then I was thunderstruck. The black body of moving objects suddenly spread out like a fan, and from it went up one single, solid yell—a war-whoop that seemed to shake the very air of the early morning. Then came the thudding roar of running horses, and the hideous cries of each of the individual warriors who were engaged in the onslaught. I could see that hundreds of Indians were coming. Had it not been for the ridge pole, all of us would have been asleep."

Dixon, thinking the Indians were merely trying to run off the horses, tied his to a wagon and reached for his gun, expecting to get off a few shots as the Indians retreated. Instead, he saw Indians heading straight for him, whipping their horses at every jump.

"There was never a more splendidly barbaric sight," he recalled later. "In after years I was glad that I had seen it. Hundreds of warriors, the flower of the fighting men of the southwestern Plains tribes, mounted upon their finest horses, armed with guns and lances, and carrying heavy shields of thick buffalo hide, were coming like the wind. Over all was splashed the rich colors of red, vermilion and ochre, on the bodies of the men, on the bodies of the running horses. [This was Isatai's supposedly bulletproof paint.] Scalps dangled from bridles, gorgeous war bonnets fluttered their plumes, bright feathers dangled from the tails and manes of the horses, and the bronzed, half-naked bodies of the riders glittered with ornaments of silver and brass. Behind this headlong charging host stretched the Plains, on whose horizon the rising sun was lifting its morning fires. The warriors seemed to emerge from this glowing background.

"I must confess, however, that the landscape possessed little interest for me when I saw that the Indians were coming to attack us, and that they would be at hand in a few moments. War-whooping had a very appreciable effect upon the roots of a man's hair."

While Dixon admired—briefly—the savage spectacle bearing down on Adobe Walls, the other denizens of the camp hastily forted up. Dixon found himself locked out of Hanrahan's Saloon and pounded on the door to be let in, feeling, he said, rather lonesome as bullets thudded all around him.

The first half-hour of the attack belonged to the Indians. The Shadler brothers and their dog were caught

"There was never a more splendidly barbaric sight," he recalled later. "In after years I was glad that I had seen it."

outside and killed; all three were scalped. The buffalo hunters, many clad only in their underwear, barricaded doors and windows with sacks of flour and grain as Indians rode right up to the buildings and struck them with their gun butts. Then a steady rain of fire rang out from the large-bore buffalo rifles, driving the Indians back.

Time and again the Indians charged to the sound of an army bugle. The bugler's identity is doubtful, but the strategy backfired. Two former soldiers were inside Hanrahan's, and they were able to tell the others when to expect an attack by listening to the bugle calls.

It quickly became apparent to the Indians that Isatai's magic paint was not working. Dead and wounded Indians littered the ground around the buildings, even though their companions made heroic efforts to carry them off. It was not a one-sided fight, however, Dixon said, "...for at times the bullets poured in like hail and made us hug the sod walls like gophers when a hawk is swooping past."

By noon ammunition ran low in Hanrahan's, and he and Dixon made a dash to Rath's store, some fifty yards away. Hanrahan returned to his store, but Dixon stayed at Rath's, where there were fewer fighters. By four o'clock the battered Indians had withdrawn to a distance, and the buffalo hunters found it safe to venture outside and compare notes. Dixon prowled about the battlefield, gathering trophies from the Indians he had killed. From one he took a silver-mounted bridle, from another a lance, from a third guns, bow, and quiver. Fifty-six dead horses and twenty-eight dead oxen littered the grounds, along with the bodies of thirteen Indians and three whites. Besides the Shadler brothers, a buffalo hunter named Billy Tyler had been killed.

As Dixon tried to sleep that night, scenes from the battle kept replaying in his head. A bewildering swirl of fantastic colors, movements, and sounds invaded his slumber. Indians charged, fired, whooped, died. Big fifty-caliber Sharps rifles thundered death. A pet crow, an omen of death, flew in and out of the buildings as bullets whistled by, cawing in a most doleful and irritating way. Frightened horses reared, plunged, and screamed when wounded.

The night itself was far more peaceful than Dixon's nightmares. The Indians made no move to attack. Their war chief, Quanah Parker, had been wounded. Isatai had been disgraced; some of the Cheyennes wanted to kill him. Despite his assurances of the magic of his paint, he had watched the battle from a safe distance; for the rest of his life he was called "that comical fellow" by other Indians.

The Battle of Adobe Walls shattered the Indians' spirit. It was obvious to even the most hopeful and desperate warrior that if 700 Indians could not defeat a handful of buffalo hunters, there was no way they were going to throw all the whites out. Still, they stayed in the area, hoping against hope they could starve the hunters out or perhaps spook them into giving up their fortress. Instead, they got another nasty surprise, and Billy Dixon became famous. Here is how he told what happened.

"On the third day a party of about fifteen Indians appeared on the edge of the bluff, east of Adobe Walls Creek, and some of the boys suggested that I try the big '50' on them. The distance was not far from seven-eighths of a mile [It was later measured at 1,583 yards]. A number of exaggerated accounts have been written about this incident. I took careful aim and pulled the trigger. We saw an Indian fall from his horse. The others dashed out of sight behind a clump of timber. A few moments later two Indians ran quickly on foot to where the dead Indian lay, seized his body and scurried to cover."

Dixon's lucky shot with the big Sharps rifle some Indians said "shoots today, kills tomorrow" helped convince the Indians to withdraw. Riders pounded away to surrounding buffalo hunters camps and to Dodge City for help, and within days over a hundred men arrived.

On the fifth day the battle claimed its last victim. William Olds was posted atop Rath's store to watch for Indians as the rest worked to fortify the buildings. As he came down the ladder into the store, his gun went off, tearing off the top of his head. His wife, who had borne the stress of battle coolly, had to deal with his death virtually uncomforted. Dixon said, "A rough lot of men, such as we were, did not know how to comfort a woman in such distress.... When we tried to speak to her we just choked up and stood still."

Dixon and a few others headed into Dodge City, where they soon put the events of the past few days behind them as they took advantage of their status as celebrities to plunder the hospitality of the saloons. "Things at Dodge were run for the fullest enjoyment of the present," Dixon commented dryly. "There was not much material to occupy students of ancient history." Some in the group, having seen enough Indians and adventure to last them their lifetimes, bought tickets to back east. Dixon signed on as a scout with the army under General Nelson Miles, a position he held for the next nine years.

The fight at Adobe Walls was over, but the Indians were not done. Separating into a number of war parties, the Indians raided into New Mexico, Colorado, and Kansas. Government reports put the number of people killed in these raids at 190. Designed to force the whites from the buffalo range, the raids backfired on the Indians even worse than the battle at Adobe Walls had. The government decided that all Indians must be forced onto reservations and kept there, and a concerted military campaign to achieve that goal was launched. The result was

the Red River War of 1874-75, in which defeat after defeat was inflicted on the Indians.

The Indians' great and final crusade had failed. As Ten Bears had said, the Texans had the country the Indians loved. Ten Bears' final wish was not granted, however. Instead of being allowed to wander on the prairies until they died, the proud Comanches were herded onto reservations. Even the most stubborn band of Comanches, under Quanah Parker, finally surrendered in June 1875, almost exactly one year after their defeat at Adobe Walls.

Billy Dixon himself later earned the Congressional Medal of Honor in the Buffalo Wallow Fight, and eventually he retired to his beloved Panhandle, where he homesteaded the site of the original Adobe Walls, just a mile or so from the site of the famous battle. He ranched, planted an extensive orchard and cottonwood trees, and grew alfalfa. Later he served as postmaster at Adobe Walls and had a small store. Ranchers took up the grassland recently grazed by the buffalo, and Dixon did quite a trade in candy and chewing gum. "No schoolgirl could be as foolish as a cowboy about candy and chewing gum," he remarked. He married and raised a family, and late in life he dictated his memoirs to his wife.

Through Olive Dixon's efforts her husband was buried at the site of the battle, and a marker to the whites who fought there was erected in 1924. The Indians arranged to have a marker put up to their fallen heroes, and the two sit side by side today in the valley. Other stones mark the sites of the graves of the Shadlers, Billy Tyler, Billy Dixon, and William Olds.

I am a sentimental sucker who blubbers his way through old cemeteries, and the marker honoring the Indian dead has an effect on me similar to one on the prairies east of Austin in an isolated, rural cemetery. Three stones mark the graves of first one child and then another of the local doctor. The final stone marks the burial place of the doctor's wife and a child, both of whom died during childbirth, quite likely despite his own efforts to save them. The inscription that tears my heart so reads simply, "Who knows what dreams lie buried here."

What dreams, indeed, lie buried at Adobe Walls. Not the dreams of one man, but the dreams of an entire people. "They died for that which make [sic] life worth living—Indian's liberty, freedom, peace —on the plains which they enjoyed for generations," the Indians' marker at Adobe Walls says.

Some feel the dream may not yet be dead. The Great Plains, they say, will revert to grassland when the aquifers below are pumped dry. Some envision turning the Great Plains into a "buffalo common," a national park where the animals can roam freely, perhaps to be pursued by descendants of those long-ago Indians who here gave their lives that the Indian dream should not perish. Perhaps the day may come again when the Indian and the buffalo live the life described in another old song:

Oh, give me a home, where the buffalo roam,

And the deer and the antelope play.

Where seldom is heard, a discouraging word,

And the skies are not cloudy all day.

It is a dream worthy of a great people, no matter what the colors of their skins.

❧ 6 ❧

Bury Me Not on the Lone Prairie

"**B**URY ME NOT ON THE LONE PRAIRIE" rightly belongs to that group of songs called folk, the body of music passed down through the generations, original authors now unknown. In this particular case, however, the tune, the mood, and many of the sentiments expressed in the song sprang not from a nameless, lonesome cowboy dying far from home but from a popular ballad, "The Ocean Burial." Written in 1839 by George Chapin and set to music by George N. Allen in 1850, "The Ocean Burial" furnished inventive prairie crooners the skeleton—and much of the meat—of one of the most popular and enduring of American folk songs. From the pitiful plea in the opening line, "Oh, bury me not in the deep, deep sea," to the disregard of the departed's wishes in the final stanza, the legacy of the earlier tune is clear:

"Oh, bury me not—"And his voice failed there;

But they gave no heed to his dying prayer;

They have lowered him slow o'er the vessel's side,

And above him was closed the dark, cold tide.

Like most folk songs, "Bury Me Not on the Lone Prairie" has perhaps as many versions as there are singers. It is in the nature of a folk song to be thus unfettered. No version is more "correct" than any other; all exist in the same way that there is no one perfect model of a human being; we all simply are what we are.

* * * * *

Bury Me Not - Dying Cowboy

Trad.
Arr. Stevens/Seyer

Oh Bur y me not. on the lone prai-

re These words came low and mourn ful

ly from the pal lid lips of a youth who

lay on his dy ing bed at the close of

day he had wailed in

Arranged by Michael Stevens

Oh bury me not on the lone praire
These words came low and mournfully
From the pallid lips of a youth who lay
On his dying bed at the close of day

He had wailed in pain till o'er his brow
Death's shadows fast were gathering now
He thought of his home and his loved ones nigh
As the cowboys gathered to see him die

Oh bury me not on the lone prairie
In the narrow grave six foot by three
Where the buffalo paws o'er a prairie sea
Oh bury me not on the lone prairie

It matters not I've oft been told
Where the body lies when the heart grows cold
Yet grant oh grant this wish to me
O bury me not on the lone prairie

O we buried him there on the lone prairie
Where the wild rose blooms and the wind blows free
O his pale young face never more to see
For we buried him there on the lone prairie

Oh bury me not on the lone prairie
Where the wild coyotes will howl o'er me
Where the rattlesnakes hiss and the crow flies free
Oh bury me not on the lone prairie

From very early times humans have shown an extraordinary interest in the circumstances of their final resting situation. Ancient peoples interred their dead with grave goods calculated to enable them to function in the afterlife much as they had done in life. Modern peoples invest heavily in waterproof vaults and gasketed caskets and are laid to rest in their finest clothes. Despite lacking concrete evidence of the necessity of these arrangements, such is the mystique of death that humans feel compelled to make an effort to deny its effects and permanence.

Humans identify strongly with places with which they are familiar. To a Bedouin wanderer born and reared in the desert, an East Texas pine forest would be as much a foreign place as it would be home to a native of the region. To Texans trailing cattle up from the South Texas Plains or the Cross Timbers or the Hill Country, the sweeping reaches of the Great Plains were as foreign and unhomelike as if they belonged to another country. Wishing to be buried among one's people, in familiar surroundings that speak of home, is a simple affirmation of the fact that, like all of us, cowboys were human. We may not know where we're headed as we start out into the Great Beyond, but we like to begin the journey from a familiar place.

The Goodnight-Loving Trail

The Goodnight-Loving Trail did not give rise to "Bury Me Not on the Lone Prairie," but it furnished one of the best-known examples of the cowboy's romantic desire to be buried, as one version of the song relates, "Where my friends can come and weep o'er me." The story of how Charles Goodnight honored the request of his dying friend Oliver Loving not to be laid away "in a foreign country" also is a fitting capstone to a partnership saga that exemplifies the qualities of honor and loyalty.

Goodnight and Loving met in the late 1850s. Goodnight and his partner Wes Sheek set up a ranch not far from the Brazos River a day's ride northwest of Weatherford, then a scattering of log cabins along the military road between Fort Worth and Fort Belknap. Loving ran a small country store on the road and ranched. Like many other Texas cowmen, he trailed herds to markets outside Texas even before the Civil War, delivering beef to Louisiana, Illinois, and Colorado.

Charles Goodnight's epic journey from Fort Sumner, New Mexico, to Weatherford, Texas, with the body of his friend Oliver Loving fulfilled one cowboy's wish to be buried "Where my friends can come and weep o'er me."

The UT Institute of Texan Cultures at San Antonio, No. 68-256

During the Civil War the western frontier of Texas was largely undefended against the Indians, and the line of settlement retreated near a hundred miles to the east. Ranches were abandoned, but much of the stock remained on the prairies, running wild. When the war ended, millions of unbranded cattle roamed Texas. They were virtually the only resource the war-battered state had that could be readily converted to cash—if they could be moved to market. Goodnight expressed the common view of the situation in Texas. "It looked like everything worth living for was gone. The entire country was depressed—there was no hope."

Texas railroads at the time linked inland areas to seaports but did not connect the state by land to the rest of the nation. Cattle came equipped with four feet, however, and the lack of rails posed no problem to cash-hungry ranchers. Cattle could walk to railheads located along the new transcontinental railroad in Kansas. (Even after railroads reached such Texas cities as Dallas and Fort Worth in later years, many cowmen preferred to continue drives to Kansas railheads. Nearer to northern markets, those cities offered lower freight rates that resulted in higher profits.) Trail driving, practiced on a small scale in Texas since Spanish times, began in earnest following the Civil War.

Ironically, Charles Goodnight, arguably the most famous trail driver, did not begin his career by taking herds up the trail to Kansas. He thought the situation over and decided that "the whole of Texas would start north for market," using the old trails established before the war. He decided to go west instead. Gold had been discovered in Colorado, and the glitter of the bright metal lured a man who'd seen Confederate money become worthless. "First, the mining region would have more or less money," he said in explaining his reasoning, "and, second, in that region there was a good cattle country, so if I could not sell I could hold."

Moving two or three thousand edgy longhorn steers (three- to five-year-old steers were preferred by buyers over cows and younger animals) some 1,500 miles through territory raided by Indians, broiled by sun in summer and frozen by blizzards in winter, making them gain weight on the way, and keeping them from being stampeded by rustlers, lightning, or the clang of a pot lid dropped by the cook was no easy job. And there was no book on the subject, even if the rancher could read. Goodnight, like other trail drivers, "wrote the book" by making it up as he went, developing by trial and error the principles of proper management of herds on the trail. Later in life Goodnight set down his methods.

"When I first made up my mind that I was going to drive, I set about collecting my outfit. My first step toward this was to round up fifty or sixty good horses. Then the mess-wagon was made ready with provisions. For instance, when the Goodnight Trail was laid off, I had to prepare for a six-hundred-mile stretch between settlements. Meantime, I informed my neighbor stockmen that I was to drive to a northern market, and would receive any cattle they wanted to go with the herd, arranging for the concentration of the herd at some given point, where the cattle were driven through a chute and branded with a trail or road brand. I was never over three days in putting the average herd of three thousand head together.

"Owing to the danger of Indians and stampede, I always got out of the settlements as soon as possible, for cattle that were scattered were much easier traced on the trail than in the settlements, and the danger of meeting Indians was less. Our outfits consisted of sixteen to eighteen men, a mess-wagon drawn by four mules, driven by the cook, and a horse wrangler who had charge of the horse herd. We aimed to have as many experienced men as possible, and after a few years there developed on the trail a class of men that could be depended upon anywhere.

"These men were thoroughly drilled regarding their places and duties. I always selected two of the most skillful to be my pointers, to handle the front of the herd and keep it on the course given out by the foreman. These were never changed from their positions at the head of the herd. I always selected three steady men for the rear, to look out for the weaker cattle—the drags. . . .

"The rest of the men were divided along the sides, the swing. Except for the corner men they were changed each morning, as the nearer the point the lighter the work, and a system of rotation divided the labor on men and horses. Besides, three hundred miles of the Pecos was bad with alkali dust, and the men not only shifted their positions daily, but reversed their sides of the herd. . . . [Riders downwind of the herd had to eat dust all day, so they took turns.]

"Trail hands were well disciplined and were governed entirely by signals, being too far from the leaders to receive orders any other way. The handling of the herd in the least time and at the least expense of horseflesh caused a system of signals to come into use—signals mostly derived from the Plains Indians and well adapted to the purpose. They were all made from horseback, and movements of the hat were the principal features.

"The signal to break camp and move upon the trail, simply a motion with the hat in the direction to be followed, was repeated by the pointers and passed along to the rear. About eleven o'clock the signal to graze was passed along the line. Then the men ate dinner, which had been prepared while breakfast was cooking. When the cattle began to lie down, the manager knew that they had grazed long enough, and gave the signal to resume the trail. . . ."

Trail herds might spend three months or more on the trail, and life settled into the daily routine Goodnight described. It was undoubtedly hot, dusty, and dull most of the time. The latter was to be desired. Calm herds made good time, put on flesh, and lessened the burdens of the cowhands. But they did not furnish exciting tales to tell the folks back home. Stampedes, hailstorms, and encounters with Indians and rustlers did, and anyone who has seen movie and television accounts might believe a trip up the trail was a daily bedlam of bolting steers and blazing Winchesters. Sometimes such things did happen, and the result was not necessarily something to brag about, but cowboys did so anyway.

One old cowboy "stretched the blanket" a bit in telling about a stampede. "In the darkness the herd headed for a sixty-foot bluff and poured over the top like hell after a preacher. I was ridin' on their fetlocks when my night horse—and God, he was a good one—went over the top with them. And I was still a-settin' in the saddle like a reg'lar hand when he hit on his all-fours and bogged three feet deep in solid rock."

W. A. Roberts came nearer the truth when he said, "Barring stampedes, and storms when balls of lightning played on the tips of our horses' ears and great balls of electricity came rolling along the ground, trail driving was a fascinating life. We have forgotten the hardships and remember only the pleasant things."

Another old-timer, G. O. Burrows, recalled some of the things Roberts forgot. "I had my share of the ups and downs —principally downs—on the old cattle trail. Some of my experiences were going hungry, getting wet and cold, riding sore-backed horses, going to sleep on herd and losing cattle, getting 'cussed' by the boss, scouting for 'gray-backs,' [lice] trying the 'sick racket' now and then to get a night's sleep, and other things too numerous to mention. . . . Have often stopped a few days in Chicago, St. Louis and Kansas City, but always had the 'big time' when I arrived in good old Santone rigged out with a pair of high-heeled boots and striped breeches, and about $6.30 worth of other clothes. Along about sundown you could find me at Jack Harris' show occupying a front seat and clamoring for the next performance. This 'big time' would last but a few days, however, for I would soon be 'busted' and would have to borrow money to get out to the ranch, where I would put in the fall and winter telling about the big things I had seen up North. The next spring I would have the same old trip, the same old things would happen in the same old way, and with the same old wind-up. I put in eighteen or twenty years on the trail, and all I had in the final outcome was the high-heeled boots, the striped pants and about $4.80 worth of other clothes, so there you are."

While the cowpuncher might gain more experience than money from a drive, the financial rewards for big drivers like Goodnight were substantial at times. After a successful drive, the rancher might head back to Texas with $20,000 or more in his saddlebags. Little wonder, then, that Goodnight tried to make the operation run as smoothly as possible. One of his innovations became a legend in cattle country: the lead steer Old Blue [see chapter 7].

"I was the only trail man I know of who used steer leaders," Goodnight recalled. "I conceived the idea after the first trip and found it to be of great

Indians, stampedes, and thirst were the deadly trinity of the trail drive. Once a herd started to run, about all cowhands could do was try to stay ahead of them—or risk being trampled.

The UT Institute of Texan Cultures at San Antonio, No. 74-947

advantage. I used two steers. The bells I put on them were of the very best type and were arranged with a strap which would easily stop the clapper. When the signal to graze was given, the man in charge of the lead steers would fasten down the clappers and turn the steers off the trail. After we had been out a month, should a clapper come loose at night the whole herd would be on its feet in no time. The lead steers were of great advantage in swimming rivers and in penning, for the cattle soon learned to go where the bell called them."

Old Blue was more than an ordinary lead steer, however. Goodnight acquired him as a three-year-old from John Chisum and trailed him up to Colorado with a herd destined to feed reservation Indians. Blue was spared that fate and was broken to the yoke. In 1877 Goodnight brought him to Texas after he moved his operation into Palo Duro Canyon following the defeat of the Comanches.

Charles Goodnight had three trail-driving partners he knew could always be counted on. Old Blue was one; Oliver Loving another; Bose Ikard the third. Fittingly, Goodnight stood by them all until the end.

Oliver Loving was Goodnight's business partner, but Bose Ikard occupied a place in Goodnight's heart above all others. "He was probably the most devoted man to me that I ever had. I have trusted him farther than any living man," Goodnight said.

Ikard went up the trail with Goodnight and Loving on their first drive in 1866 and was a regular fixture thereafter. Ikard was the cowboy's cowboy. He could climb onto the "hurricane deck" of a knot-headed pony and ride him into the ground. He was especially skilled at night-herding duty. Goodnight described the events of a stampede on a drive in 1867 in which Bose displayed his exceptional cow sense and riding skills.

"Something happened, in an instant the herd stampeded right down on the camp, and it looked as though the men would be trampled to death. There certainly was some scrambling, as most of them had not got out of bed," Goodnight recalled. "I jerked a blanket off one of the beds, jumped in front of the cattle that were coming at full speed, and by waving the blanket and doing all the yelling I could, succeeded in splitting the herd around the wagon and beds." Goodnight then leaped on his horse and took out after the herd, trying to get in front of them and turn them.

"By this time it was light enough to see. I kept going up the side of the cattle as fast as possible, wondering why Bose had not turned the front. When I had almost caught up with him, he looked back and saw me, and immediately his horse shot out like lightning and he threw the leaders around. After we got them circled, I asked him why he had not turned them sooner."

The herd had already been stampeded by Indians, and Ikard had not been able to determine the cause of this run. "I'll tell you, sir," he said. "I wasn't certain who had this herd until I saw you. I thought maybe the Indians had them." Still, Ikard stayed with the herd in spite of the possible danger to his life.

Such events make it clear why Goodnight said Ikard "surpassed any man I had in endurance and stamina. There was a dignity, a cleanliness, and a reliability about him that was wonderful.... His behavior was very good in a fight.... He was my detective, banker, and everything else in Colorado, New Mexico, and the other wild country I was in. The nearest and only bank was at Denver, and when we carried money I gave it to Bose....

> Such events make it clear why Goodnight said Ikard "surpassed any man I had in endurance and stamina ...

"We went through some terrible trials during those four years on the trail. While I had a good constitution and endurance, after being in the saddle for several days and nights, on various occasions, and finding I could stand it no longer, I would ask Bose if he would take my place, and he never failed to answer me in the most cheerful and willing manner...."

Good men, like good horses, do wear out eventually, and Bose Ikard was no exception. As both grew old, Ikard sometimes sent word to Goodnight that he needed money, and Goodnight never let his old friend down. Ikard died in 1929 and was buried at Weatherford. Just before his own death, Goodnight had a marker erected over Ikard's grave, with the following inscription: "Bose Ikard. Served with me four years on the Goodnight-Loving Trail, never shirked a duty or disobeyed an order, rode with me in many stampedes, participated in three engagements with Comanches, splendid behavior."

Two more facts need to be understood to appreciate fully the high regard in which Charles Goodnight held Bose Ikard: Bose Ikard was black, and the Civil War had ended just one year before he went to work for Goodnight. Ikard had been born a slave. He was one of a large number of former slaves turned cowboys who helped drive herds up the trail while the black troopers known as the buffalo soldiers were defeating the Comanches and Apaches. Most people have conveniently forgotten —if they ever knew—the role blacks like Bose Ikard played in winning the west, but Charles Goodnight, one of the most prominent white players in that drama, never forgot. And unlike many lesser men of his and later times, Goodnight did not let the shade of a man's skin color his opinion of the person.

101

Goodnight and Loving decided to partner for their first drive in 1866. They threw their herds together and headed out from Fort Belknap on June 6 with two thousand cattle, eighteen men, and the "mess-wagon" Goodnight had cobbled together from the running gear of a government freight wagon. On the rear he had a local woodworker build a box with a hinged rear lid that let down onto a swinging leg to form a worktable. Goodnight's chuck wagon was copied extensively, and the design is basically unaltered today.

In 1866 the Great Plains of the Texas Panhandle were mysterious territory, little explored. In addition, they were the range of the buffalo and the Plains Indians, principally Comanches and Kiowas. Goodnight had served many years as a scout for Texas rangers chasing Indians onto the plains, and he knew the area well enough to have struck directly northwest to Colorado. However, he knew that anyone doing so would be lucky to cross the plains in possession of both cattle and scalp, and he elected not to make the attempt.

Instead, Goodnight and Loving chose to take the long way around, by heading south from Fort Belknap, picking up the Pecos River and following it to the foot of the Rocky Mountains, and then moving north parallel to the mountains. Their ultimate objective on their early drives was Fort Sumner, New Mexico, where the government was buying beef to feed Indians on nearby reservations. The distance was twice as far as the direct route, but success was more likely.

The route was not without its hazards. The Horsehead Crossing of the Pecos was notably treacherous for several reasons. The approach was across a desert stretching some eighty waterless miles from the Concho River. The herd would have to travel several days without water, and when they drew near and scented water, they were likely to stampede for it and trample each other. Quicksand bogs could swallow hundreds of cattle, and alkali ponds along the stream could kill in minutes anything that drank from them. In addition, the Horsehead Crossing was used by Indians, and a meeting with them could mean a fight and perhaps loss of some or all of the herd.

Goodnight and Loving learned of several of these hazards on their first drive. Herds usually traveled twelve to fifteen miles a day and drank daily. Goodnight and Loving pushed the herd hard and bedded them without water, and the cattle didn't like it. They milled around all night long, requiring the efforts of the whole crew to hold them. Goodnight realized that if the cattle were going to be walking all night they might as well be making progress toward water, and after the first night the drive never stopped. Goodnight and Loving and crew were in the saddle for three days and nights without sleep. When the cattle did smell water they broke, went over ten-foot banks, and many drowned. Others drank alkali water and died. For two full days the cursing hands dragged bogged cattle out of quicksand and altogether over 400 head were lost.

Having learned their lesson, on future drives Goodnight watered the cattle well on the Concho and then pushed them day and night, pausing to graze a couple of times but not stopping until they reached the Pecos. Goodnight recalled that the cattle "were difficult to handle, but we never lost a head after learning this system of crossing the Plains."

The partners learned to deal with the desert, but the Indians were an altogether different proposition. The Comanches quickly picked up the trail of their first drive, and thereafter these opportunistic raiders were a constant threat. Sometimes they stampeded herds and got away with only a few head; at other times they took entire herds and sometimes a few scalps as well.

Oliver Loving met his death at the hands of the Comanches during a drive in 1867. Indians bedeviled the drovers almost from the time they began the drive in Texas, stampeding the herd at night twice in as many days. The next night half the spooked herd began to run again, this time in circles around the half that did not run, keeping on until their tongues were hanging out. A fierce electrical storm attacked, and the cattle finally ran

themselves down, to the relief of the cowboys who had not slept in three nights.

The drive was off to a terrible start, and it got worse. This herd seemed born to run, and it did so again and again. During one stampede Goodnight saved the outfit by waving a blanket at cattle about to run down the camp; they split and went around at the last minute while swearing cowboys struggled to get out of their bedrolls and into their saddles. At the Pecos the cattle ran again, and Indians got part of them.

The troubles delayed the drive, and Loving decided to go ahead so as to be present in Santa Fe when new government contracts were let. He took "One-Armed" Wilson with him, and they set off, traveling at night to avoid being spotted by Indians.

After seeing no Indians for days, Loving decided to risk riding by day, and the decision cost him his life. Near the Guadalupe Mountains, Indians gave chase and pursued them to the Pecos, where the two took refuge in a ditch in the riverbed. Several hundred Indians surrounded them, and a desperate fight began. Wilson and Loving killed several, and finally the Indians proposed a truce, speaking in Spanish. No sooner had Wilson stepped from cover to talk, however, when an Indian sent a bullet into Loving's wrist and side.

The siege resumed, with Wilson and Loving cowering in the ditch while the

Indians rained arrows on them, shooting high into the air so the arrows would fall almost vertically into the ditch. Wilson and Loving hugged the side of the ditch nearest the Indians and managed to avoid being hit.

Loving was suffering considerably from his wounds, and he persuaded Wilson to make a run for it and go to Goodnight for help. Wilson arrayed their five six-shooters and a rifle so Loving could reach them with his good arm, stripped down to his hat, drawers, and undershirt, and slipped away into the stream.

The pair had expected Goodnight to be some forty miles away, but he had stopped to rest the herd for a day and a half and was nearly eighty miles distant. When Wilson reached the herd, Goodnight described him as "the most terrible object I ever saw. His eyes were wild and bloodshot, his feet were swollen beyond all reason, and every step he took left blood in the track."

Goodnight and five others set out immediately to find Loving. All night they pressed on through a pouring rain. When they reached the site of the battle they charged, fully expecting to have to shoot their way in to Loving. To their surprise, the place was deserted. Loving's hiding place was clearly marked by a hundred or so holes where arrows had lodged, but signs showed Goodnight the Indians had not found Loving.

After waiting two days and nights for rescue, all the while holding the Indians at bay, Loving had crawled into the water at night and headed upstream. On the third day freighters found him, fed him, and agreed to take him to Fort Sumner, about 150 miles to the north.

Goodnight, meanwhile, had given his friend up for dead. He learned differently some days later as the herd neared Fort Sumner.

As a measure of how rough the trip had been, Goodnight had not slept in his bedroll for thirty-two nights past. He slept on his horse ("You got to where you could sleep on a horse without any trouble," he said.) or napped while propped against a wheel of the chuck wagon. Yet such was his regard for Loving that he immediately set out to ride the remaining 110 miles between him and his friend. He made the ride in approximately twenty-four hours without stopping to rest.

Unfortunately, gangrene attacked Loving's arm soon after, and it had to be amputated. Loving began to go downhill soon after, and he called his friend Goodnight in for a talk. As a result of selling cattle to the defunct Confederacy, Loving was deeply in debt. Goodnight agreed to continue their partnership even after Loving's death, until all his partner's debts were paid. Then Loving broached a subject that weighed even heavier on his mind.

"I regret I have to be laid away in a foreign country," he told Goodnight.

"I assured him that he need have no fears; that I would see that his remains were laid in the cemetery at home. He felt that this would be impossible, but I told him it would be done. He died September 25, 1867, and was temporarily buried at Sumner," Goodnight said.

Once the herd had been disposed of, Goodnight turned to keeping his final promise to Loving. He had his hands gather discarded oil cans from the fort dump ground and beat them out flat. Then the cans were soldered together into an oversized tin casket. Loving was exhumed, and, still inside his wooden casket, was packed in powdered charcoal, sealed up, and crated in wood. Thus he made his final trip down the trail that he and his partner had blazed and that still bears their names. Larry McMurtry borrowed freely from this tale when he wrote *Lonesome Dove.*

It's tempting to think that somewhere along the trail back to Texas, Goodnight and the boys passed some time reminiscing about their late friend, and after a respectful silence a cowboy sitting around the campfire pulled a harmonica out of his saddlebags and entertained the moon and the coyotes with a sorrowful rendition of "Bury Me Not on the Lone Prairie."

Maybe it happened; maybe it didn't. But I like to think it did. The moon, the coyotes, and Oliver Loving would have enjoyed it.

7

Old Blue and Sancho

THE OLD JOKE IS THAT A CAMEL IS A horse put together by a committee. The Texas longhorn is a deer put together by history. It is no more a milch cow than a French poodle is a hunting dog. It is an animal superbly adapted to its place and time.

What do you do when you're going on a long camping trip? You take along a lot of food. Spanish explorers did the same, but since they did not have freeze-dried ice cream, canned chili, and dehydrated potatoes, they took their larder along alive. Herds of cattle, horses, and sheep were standard equipage for any expedition worthy of the name. And just like the package of noodles that eludes capture in the food box and never gets eaten, not every cow disappeared down a conquistador's gullet.

Escapees from these early cattle herds formed the foundation of the longhorn breed, but other brood stock came from a variety of places. It was the mixture of wild Spanish cattle with breeds brought by Anglo settlers that finally became the Texas longhorn. The longhorn was an accident, pure and simple.

As befits the animal that became the icon of Texas, everything about the longhorn was big. Tails were so long they sometimes dragged the ground. Legs like stilts propped the longhorns up in the sky. Horns spread—and spread, and spread. A full-grown bull could weigh near a ton and have headgear eight feet wide.

As racehorses are bred for speed, longhorns were bred for mean. Running wild in the thickets along South Texas rivers and creeks, longhorns survived by whipping anything that tried to eat them, capture them, or get between them and a comely cow. Sometimes it was a grizzly bear or mountain lion; sometimes it was a person; sometimes it was another longhorn.

The bulls were especially prone to violence, so standard practice was to castrate male calves. The resulting steers were more docile, although few could have been classified as lap cows. Some, however, proved so singular in their character that they gained themselves a place in history. Two such were Sancho and Old Blue.

* * * * *

Charles Goodnight conceived the idea of using lead steers to manage trail herds. Old Blue proudly took his place at the fore and pointed his nose at the north star.

The UT Institute of Texan Cultures at San Antonio, No. 75-530

Two Texas Steers

by Michael Stevens
arr. Stevens/Seyer

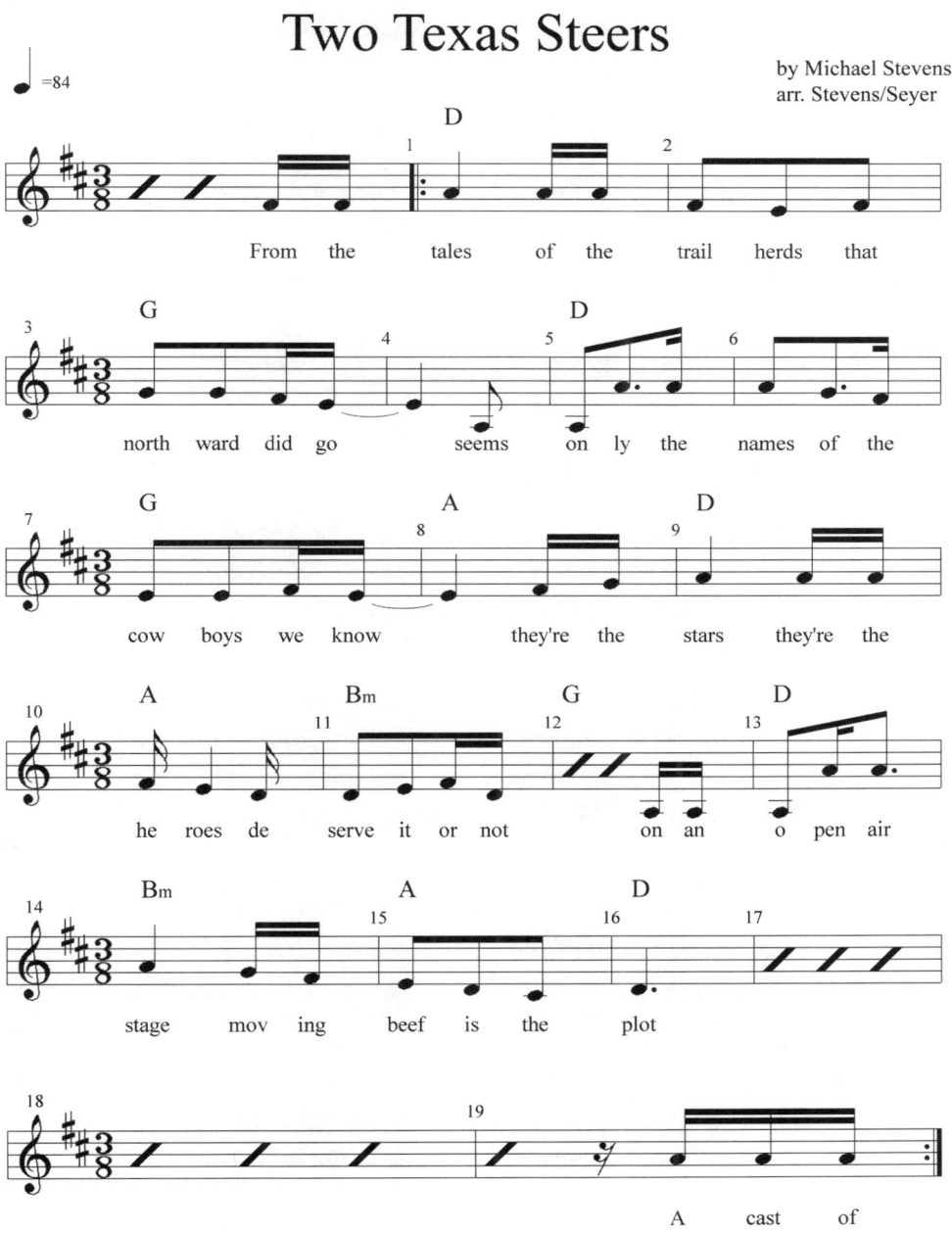

From the tales of the trail herds that

north ward did go seems on ly the names of the

cow boys we know they're the stars they're the

he roes de serve it or not on an o pen air

stage mov ing beef is the plot

A cast of

Two Texas Steers (Old Blue and Sancho)

By Michael Stevens

From the tales of the trail herds that northward did go
Seems only the names of the cowboys we know
They're the stars, they're the heroes, deserve it or not
On an open-air stage, moving beef is the plot

A cast of thousands were gathered at the old cattle call
Bit players at best with no names at all
All these extras were the cattle, the meat of the play
Nameless horns in the crowd, forgotten today

But Sancho and Blue, as they came to be known
A black and white orphan and a big ole blue roan
Two rare individuals helped open the west
And the stories of their travels are some of the best

Sancho's mamma died bogged as a water hole shrank
To his rescue and adoption, Mr. Kerr he could thank
And Maria Kerr for his weird choice of cuisine
Piloncillo, tamales, and chile pequin

What a life Sancho had for two or three years
Then driven to Wyoming, just one of the steers
That's not the end of the legend he earned
Who knows how he did it, but in spring he returned

His hooves were worn down, but he wasn't lame
This homing longhorn, Sancho's his name
And Maria so happy, she hugged him and cried
And he dined on tamales 'til the day that he died

Charlie Goodnight, pushing cattle to Colorado
Bought Blue from John Chisum in New Mexico
Ole Blue took the lead spot, he seemed to know
What the point riders wanted, and just where to go

Story goes how young Blue took an arrow in the rear
Right then stuck with a notion to be a lead steer
His savvy was noticed, needless to say
He was pulled from the sale, not shipped away

Soon Mr. Goodnight gave him a bell
Like the pied-piper fable, herds followed the spell
Some may cry Judas, with emotions overwrought
He's just a cow with an instinct, no malice aforethought

A smart critter, this steer, from the day he was born
In no time he noticed the cow ponies ate corn
So at day's end to the wagon, tryin' his luck
Soon his palate expanded to all kinds of chuck

Now I can't quite explain this unusual desire
Of not one, but two bovines who dined at man's fire
So I shall but report that this big ole blue steer
Mooched biscuits and prunes and, hell, probably beer

For eight years he helped Charlie, then his trailin' was through
To the J.A.'s in Palo Duro, retirement for Blue
At age 20, he died, this tale comes to the end
Of a cowman and a blue steer, his faithful old friend

But Sancho and Blue, as they came to be known
A black and white orphan and a big ole blue roan
Two rare individuals helped open the west
And the stories of their travels are some of the best

As an item of commerce the longhorn is rivaled in Texas history only by oil. The parallels between the two are many and striking. Both were, in effect, a natural resource waiting for exploitation by people willing to take risks. The market at home for both was small, but both were in great demand outside Texas's borders. Pipelines delivered the oil, cattle trails the beef, and the Chisholm Trail was as familiar to ranchers as the Big Inch is to wildcatters. Supplying meat and oil to the masses made fortunes for the few; the truly great Texas fortunes were built on both. Both the pump jack and the longhorn became Texas icons. They helped define who we are even as they were helping make us who we are.

J. Frank Dobie described the impact of the four-footed traffic out of Texas after the Civil War. "The Chisholm Trail was a canal out of the mighty dammed-up reservoir of Texas beef to meat-lacking consumers with money to buy.

"...The Chisholm Trail was a lane opening out of a vast breeding ground swarming with cattle life to a vacant, virgin range of seemingly illimitable expanse. It initiated the greatest, the most extraordinary, the most stupendous, the most fantastic and fabulous migration of animals controlled by man that the world has ever known or ever can know. During the seventies the Plains Indians were all being killed off or rounded up; at the same time the buffalo were all but annihilated. An empire of grass awaited occupation...."

An empire needs emperors, and in their own way longhorns like Old Blue and Sancho filled that role, too—with style.

Old Blue and Sancho

Old Blue started off the way all longhorns did—as a lustful gleam in the eye of a ground-pawing bull down in the South Texas brush country along the Nueces River. It was the summer of 1869. In the spring of the following year Old Blue's mother, heavy with calf, sought out a secluded patch of thorny brush that could be defended against all comers and dropped a gangly calf.

Little is known about Old Blue's early years, but it is likely he shared the childhood accidentally discovered by a cowboy who followed a stream of cows away from a creek. "...I noticed half a dozen dun and brindle Texas cows, who had already slaked their thirst, traveling steadily away from the water in the same direction as myself. A few young heifers and steers accompanied them, though the mass of the cattle, as I well knew, would stay by the water till the heat of the day was over; but this party of long-horned, long-legged Texas ladies clearly had business elsewhere.... An old brindle cow with rings out to the end of her horns was leading the travelers.... They struck into one of the innumerable cattle trails leading from the high pastures to the water and pressed up it, traveling one close behind the other at a steady walk that occasionally became a trot. I rode parallel to them, curious to see the goal they were making for so eagerly.

"Up we went into the high rolling sand-hills, and there, in the middle of them, in a little cup-like hollow, I saw a regular nursery. Eight little dun-coloured Texas calves lay there, squatted close to the sandy ground which their coats matched so well, their heads lying out flat, with the chins pressed down on the sand, just as little antelope fawns would have crouched. In this pose they were all but invisible. Beside them lay two elderly Texas cows, whose office had been to guard the créche.

"The mothers, who had travelled till now in perfect silence, began to low loudly and lovingly when they caught sight of their offspring, and in a moment each young hopeful had jumped up and rushed to his own dam, where his wriggling tail and nuzzling head, the busy lips frothing with milk, soon showed he was getting the dinner he had waited for so patiently. Meantime the two guardian cows had risen to their feet, and lost no time in starting off in their turn to make their trip to the water...."

At age three Blue—not yet old and still just a nameless face in a bovine sea—plodded up the Goodnight-Loving Trail to New Mexico, where he was sold to rancher John Chisum. One day he was found wandering with an Apache arrow in his rump. He was roped, thrown, and doctored, and he survived.

Charles Goodnight bought Blue when the steer was four years old, threw him with 2,500 others into a trail herd, and drove to Colorado. By this time Blue's natural leadership qualities were coming to the fore. Every morning he took a spot at the head of the herd—the point—and remained there all day. Strong, tranquil, and intelligent, he proved to be worth a dozen hands as he led the herd according to the directions of the point men. He quickly became a favorite of the cowboys, and Goodnight made a decision he never regretted. Rather than sending Blue to feed reservation Indians, he held the big steer back when the herd was sold and took him back to Colorado.

In 1874 Ranald Mackenzie defeated the Comanche Indians in their Palo Duro Canyon stronghold in the Texas Panhandle. Two years later Goodnight trailed a herd of cattle from Colorado to stock the first ranch in that part of the state. Old Blue led the herd on this historic journey.

Goodnight then made Blue his lead steer for trail drives to Kansas, and the mature longhorn seemed not only to take pride in his work, but to understand it as well. Goodnight conceived the idea of putting a bell on Blue to help guide the steers behind. The big blue steer had been proud-stepping before, but now he fairly burst with pride. "Look here, look here, look here," it seemed to toll as Blue ambled along. As far as he was concerned, he might as well have been wearing a crown and a sign proclaiming him the Lord of the Longhorns.

Each day he guided the herd north, and when the herd was thrown off the trail to graze and then bed down for the night, a cowboy tied down the clapper of Old Blue's bell. When it was time to head'em up and move'em out next morning, the herd scrambled to its feet at the clang of the bell.

Old Blue knew he was special, and he did not waste his off-duty hours hobnobbing with inferior critters from back in the herd. As soon as the clapper was tied down, Old Blue took out for camp. He headed for the chuck wagon and dined on shelled corn like the horses, but unlike them he then hung around the chuck wagon mooching sourdough biscuits, steak, prunes, and other such goodies from the cook, who had to take care lest Old Blue help himself to the cowboys' supper still cooking in the skillets. He

didn't get left out, though. The cowboys loved having Old Blue around and fed him off their plates as they ate.

If anyone doubted Old Blue's worth, those doubts were washed away on his first drive to Kansas. When they reached the Cimarron River in Oklahoma, it was roiling and foaming bank full. Old Blue never broke stride but struck straight into the water, the herd following. While six cowboys recrossed the river to help bring the chuck wagon across, Old Blue was making a big circle around the herd. When the chuck wagon emerged dripping from the water, Old Blue was standing there waiting for it. He was ready for his supper, and he'd earned it.

Disaster almost struck just south of the final destination, Dodge City, Kansas. Around midnight a howling norther drove sleet and snow into the herd, and it took every cowboy to keep the cattle from turning tail to the wind and heading back to the Palo Duro. At dawn a cowboy untied the clapper on Old Blue's bell.

There was one more river to cross— the Arkansas—and it was so cold the river had partly frozen. The cattle burst out of the icy water on the run, trying to get warm, and Old Blue had all he could do to keep his position at the head of the mob. Then he really showed his intelligence. He aimed straight for the twenty-foot gate into the shipping pens. By noon two thousand steers were on a train to Chicago and Old Blue was munching down on hay while the cowboys did what trail-weary cowboys did after reaching a town with whiskey, women, and song.

Old Blue returned to the ranch in Palo Duro Canyon and took up his other duties. Outlaw steers could hide out in the breaks for years, and when they were caught, wild was a mild word for them. Such renegades were necked to Old Blue, who would lead or, if necessary, drag the critter to camp. Once he went along on an expedition to capture some buffaloes on the plains and bring them back to the canyon. After traveling several days, two young buffaloes were tied to Blue, who took out for home. Every time he reached a spot where the party had camped on the way out, he stopped, and there they camped whether they wanted to or not. By the time the buffaloes reached the

Old Blue excelled at leading herds in dangerous situations such as river crossings.

The UT Institute of Texan Cultures at San Antonio, No. 68-303

Palo Duro Canyon, Old Blue had them minding quite well.

Old Blue spent eight years on the trail guiding herds, sometimes making two trips a year. Charles Russell said that "The confidence a steer's got in the dark is mighty frail," but Old Blue would have none of that. If the herd stampeded, Old Blue stepped to one side and let his foolish fellows run. Then he would help mold the scattered bunches back into a cohesive herd again. When the herd reached the Kansas shipping point and began shying from the pens, Old Blue would start bawling and lure them into the pens, then step aside as they were loaded into the cars.

Goodnight retired Old Blue to Palo Duro Canyon after the trail drives ended, and he died at age twenty after quite a

Old Blue was so intelligent that when it came time to load the herd into railroad cars, he would lead the cattle to the chute, then step aside. His horns now hang in the Panhandle-Plains Museum in Canyon, just a few miles from his retirement home in Palo Duro Canyon.

The UT Institute of Texan Cultures at San Antonio, No. 68-305

few years of leisure and admiring petting by all who knew him. His horns adorn the Panhandle Plains Museum in Canyon today.

Goodnight never forgot Old Blue. When J. Frank Dobie visited with the rancher, then an old man, he brought up the subject of Old Blue. "When I evidenced lively interest in Old Blue, Mr. Goodnight's spirits rose. While he would not give half of a damn for anything that anybody might write about Charlie Goodnight, he would 'like to have Old Blue given his dues.' Out of the rich stores of his memory he related instance after instance of the old Longhorn's behavior; he gave me a biographical sketch of him that he had written in doggerel verse. Back in Austin, I wrote the story of Old Blue as best I could and sold it to a magazine published in New York. After I sent Mr. Goodnight the story as printed, he responded, 'My eyes filled with tears when I read what you had written of my faithful old friend.'"

Old Blue was what Dobie called a "returner," a critter so imbued with love for its home that it always came back. Sancho was another famous returner.

Like Old Blue, Sancho first sniffed the smell of dewy grass in South Texas. In 1877 a rancher named Kerr found

> Goodnight retired Old Blue to Palo Duro Canyon after the trail drives ended, and he died at age twenty after quite a few years of leisure and admiring petting by all who knew him.

one of his cows bogged down and dead in a waterhole. Beside it, half starved, was a muddy little black-and-white bull calf, just a few days old and too weak to walk. Kerr took the waif home to his wife, María, who was in charge of raising orphans.

Soon Kerr found a cow with a young calf, and by some patient work and perseverance, he and María got the cow to adopt Sancho, as he came to be called. Keeping the two calves penned ensured the mother cow would return to suckle them each evening, but two growing calves need a lot of milk, and María, of generous proportions and childless, divined that Sancho needed a little extra smackerel to tide him over between tilts at the teat. So she began feeding Sancho the shucks from the tamales she and her husband ate. Sancho thought those were pretty fine groceries, and the next thing he knew, María was feeding him shucks with the tamale still inside.

Sancho was grazing by now, and grass seemed downright blah compared to the spicy Mexican food he was used to. Browsing down along the creek one day, Sancho spied some tiny, round, bright red, berry-looking things on a bush. He decided to try some, and in short order he was hooked on the hottest wild peppers in Texas, the chile pequin. Wild turkeys sometimes gorge on these peppers until their flesh is almost too hot to eat, but Sancho found the peppers just right. From then on he looked for them.

Sancho recognized his special status as María's pet, but he found he couldn't get away with just anything. He found himself banished from the corn patch, but María soothed his injured feelings with lumps of the brown sugar called *piloncillo*. He had a favorite mesquite tree just outside the yard gate of the house, and there he slept at night and chewed his cud during the day. He was a house steer, no doubt about it.

When he was three years old Sancho was rounded up with his brethren and sold to the Shiner brothers, who were making up three herds to take to Wyoming. Sancho was road-branded 7Z like the rest and put on the trail with the first outfit to leave.

Old Blue stayed at the head of his herd; Sancho stayed at the rear of his. From there he could clearly hear one of María's tamales calling him. Before the first night on the trail was over, every cowboy in the outfit knew they had to watch that big black-and-white steer, because he wanted to go home. He was as gentle as a Quaker nurse and as stubborn as a lawyer working on percentage, so finally the cowboys just started tying him to a bush every night.

Tying Sancho stopped his walking at night, but he still tried to head south during the day. When the herd reached the hilly, brushy country around the Llano River northwest of San Antonio, Sancho finally slipped off unnoticed and made tracks south, dreaming of María's tamales and the chile pequin peppers along Esperanza Creek.

Two days later Sancho met the second Shiner herd heading north, and the 7Z blazoned on his side made him a marked steer. The cowboys hazed him into the herd, where he immediately assumed the rearmost spot. Some nights later there was a stampede—whether Sancho started it is not known—and guess which one of the steers could not be located afterward.

But Sancho had yet to make his getaway. The third Shiner herd came along a few days later and scooped him up again. Apparently Sancho decided about this time to play along, and he stopped making trouble and running away. But he looked south often, waiting for his chance. Meanwhile, the herd snaked its way into the Indian Territory, across Kansas and Nebraska, and finally into Wyoming. It was September, it was cold, and a little fiery something in the belly would feel right nice.

Sancho didn't believe for a minute that the line in the song that promised dogies "Wyoming may be your new home" applied to him. However, the Shiner outfit turned over their herd to its new owners and headed back to Texas.

The next spring some of the Shiner cowboys were out gathering cattle along Esperanza Creek near the Kerr place when they saw a sight that made them rub their eyes. It was a black-and-white steer with a 7Z brand. They rode over to Kerr's to find out if they had seen a ghost.

"Yes," Kerr said, "Old Sancho got in about six weeks ago. His hoofs were worn mighty nigh down to the hair, but he wasn't lame. I thought María was going out of her senses, she was so glad to see him. She actually hugged him and she cried and then she begun feeding him hot

Sancho spent his golden years hanging around a South Texas ranch home much like this one, mooching tamales and sugar.

The UT Institute of Texan Cultures at San Antonio, No. 88-85

tamales. She's made a batch of them nearly every day since, just to pet that steer. When she's not feeding him tamales, she's giving him *piloncillo."*

The Shiners decided right then and there that if Sancho loved his home enough to walk back all the way from Wyoming, he deserved to stay there till he died. And he did, munching on tamales and peppers and *piloncillo* and generally being fat and happy.

Cattle are like people: Both have to be pretty special to have a song written about them. Sancho and Old Blue earned theirs.

8

The Butterfield Overland Mail

ONE OF MY FAVORITE TOWNS IN WEST TEXAS is Fort Davis, and I know I'm not alone in that preference. In addition to some of the nicest people you'll meet anywhere, the physical setting comes near being unmatched in Texas. (I live in the Hill Country, which I consider to be the prettiest part of the state, so consider that a high compliment.)

Fort Davis basks in mountain air at near a mile in altitude, which makes its climate what flowery-tongued writers of long ago used to term *salubrious*, but I will restrain myself and simply state that the difference between an August evening in Houston and in Fort Davis is of a magnitude that would strain any writer to describe. The town sits in a pleasant little valley through which wanders Limpia Creek, and that Spanish word meaning *clear, clean,* or *free* sums up not only the look and feel of the place but also the character of the people. Oh, I'm sure

there's a grump or two in town, but I haven't met them.

The water brought the army to town in 1854, the site being chosen because of its "salubrious climate and pure water." (See, I told you about that word.) There was already evidence of inhabitation there, the site being known as Painted Comanche Camp. Buffalo soldiers stationed at Fort Davis played a leading role in the defeat of the Indians in West Texas.

Fort Davis also happened to be on the main southern route to California, and the little town so quiet now once rang with the cries and cracking whips of ox team drivers, Forty-Niners, and settlers looking to see what was on the other side of Sleeping Lion Mountain (turns out it was Sawtooth Mountain, among others). Thus it fell out that when a transcontinental stage line to carry the mail between east and west coasts was established in 1858, Fort Davis was right on the way.

Butterfield Stage

by Michael Stevens
arr. Stevens/Seyer

The But ter field line was the

first to haul both peo ple and the coun try's mail

from the Miss is sip pi to the

west ern coast ac ross an o'ver land

trail the jour ney was tough and the

meals were rough as the roads and the sta tion

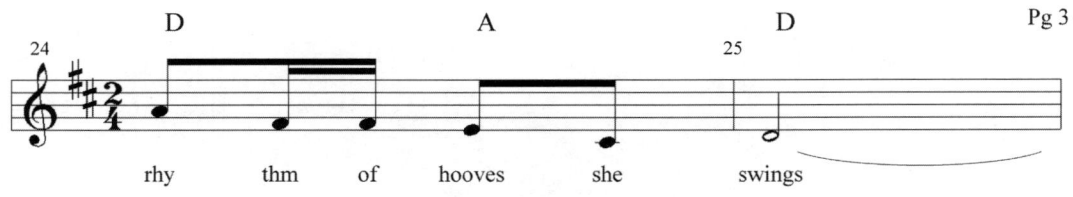

rhy   thm   of   hooves   she   swings

That

The Butterfield line was the first to haul
Both people and the country's mail
From the Mississippi to the western coast
Across an overland trail

The journey was tough and the meals were rough
As the roads and the station crews
Twenty-five days on a Concord stage
Not a trip for the weak and frail

The Butterfield stage, she rattles along
Wood wheels and leather springs
At the crack of a whip giddy-up, gee haw
With a rhythm of hooves, she swings

That grueling swing through Texas
Had the longest runs of all
Between water holes and the army forts
And mountains that are tall

From the Red River banks to Hueco Tanks
A short jaunt to Franklin Pass
Only trail through the Rocky Mountains
Didn't have much snow at all

The Butterfield stage, she rattles along
Wood wheels and leather springs
At the crack of a whip giddy-up, gee haw
With a rhythm of hooves, she swings

The Butterfield run was throttled down
By the war of the blue and gray
Then the railroads came, and the telegraph, too
The need had gone away

Faster than sail why they carried the mail
A big job they had to do
Tied a growing nation together
Helped carry it on its way

The Butterfield stage, she rattles along
Wood wheels and leather springs
At the crack of a whip giddy-up, gee haw
With a rhythm of hooves, she swings

The stage route cut across the southeast corner of what was in 1858 a military post and is now Fort Davis National Monument. Just an emphysemic mule-bray away is a museum dedicated to the Overland Trail. The 36-mile stretch of Texas 17 between Balmorhea and Fort Davis gets my vote for the prettiest stretch of highway in Texas. The road follows the valley of Limpia Creek for about twenty of those miles, winding back and forth across the creek, hemmed in by sheer walls of rich-hued stone. I hope those early riders on the stage weren't so jarred by the rocks they couldn't appreciate it.

Fort Davis is also one of my favorite places because some of the nicest people not just in West Texas but in the world, period, own and operate the Hotel Limpia in "downtown" Fort Davis—Joe and Lanna Duncan.

Joe Duncan's family first arrived in the Fort Davis area in 1883. "My great-grandfather ranched north of town," Joe said. "He and his brothers owned most of the land between Fort Stockton and Fort Davis. My father hated ranching, since he grew up in it, so he got a teaching degree and taught school in Fort Davis. He was the superintendent here for about fifteen years."

Joe's father was instrumental in preserving the old buildings in town and in the nearby fort. He bought the Hotel Limpia, and while working there one summer, Joe met a schoolteacher turned waitress for the summer named Lanna Tweedy. Lanna's parents had come to Fort Davis on their honeymoon, fell in love (with the town), and helped restore some of the buildings at the fort, living there for a time. They moved away for twenty-five years but now own the Stone Village Motel, just down the street from the Hotel Limpia.

Joe and Lanna were married in front of the ruins of the Fort Davis chapel, just a toss of a wedding bouquet from where the Overland Mail stages once rumbled through. After living eight years in Dallas, Fort Davis called them home, and they bought the hotel and moved back home. Their first step was to buy the twenty-nine rocking chairs that line the hotel porch.

The Duncans still use replicas of the original hotel stationery, complete with advertising slogans such as "Not where the West begins but where the West is." "The finest place anywhere for children and run down mothers." "Good home cooking." None of those things have changed.

Today Lanna and Joe and Mancha (Spot) the dog and Gato (Cat) the cat figuratively hold down the fort at Fort Davis. And if you sit on the hotel porch about sunset, rock real easy, and listen real hard, you just might hear the crack of a stage driver's whip and the rumble of steel-rimmed wheels along the old route of the Overland Mail.

Fort Davis just may have occupied the prettiest spot ever chosen for a frontier fort in Texas, the mouth of Limpia Canyon. The ruins at the present-day site date from the second, post-Civil War occupation of the fort and sit farther from the mouth of the canyon than the first buildings.

The UT Institute of Texan Cultures at San Antonio, No. 72-327

127

The Butterfield Overland Mail

Passenger and mail service by stagecoach from east coast to west was an idea whose time was almost already past. It still took months for ships to sail around South America from New York to San Francisco, but even as the Overland Mail was aborning, so were technological innovations that would soon have supplanted it. The Transcontinental Railroad and telegraph were just a few years away, and faster steam-powered ships were already plying the nation's waters.

However, the Overland Mail offered something that none of the others—save the railroad—could offer: Local point-to-point service across the nation in addition to through service from coast to coast.

Several factors had to be taken into account in planning a route. Foremost was the fact that at this point the vast midsection of the country, the Great Plains, was still considered to be an impenetrable desert. Too, the area was the domain of the buffaloes, the Comanches, and other Indian tribes. Since regular year round service was desired, a route had to be chosen that would avoid the snow-closed passes of the Rocky Mountains in winter. That dictated a southern route.

Routing the coaches across Texas offered several advantages as well as posing some difficulties. There was a string of United States forts across the breadth of Texas that could offer protection from Indians over much of the route. Rivers in Texas generally all run from northwest to southeast. This meant both problems in fording many streams as well as opportunities for locating way stations near water. At the tiny village of Franklin, opposite the Mexican town of El Paso del Norte, lay the southernmost snow-free pass across the Rockies.

In March 1857 Congress passed legislation authorizing a mail contract calling for the carrying of letter mail on a twice weekly schedule, in four-horse coaches suitable for passengers, from St. Louis to San Francisco. The act called for the trip to be made within twenty-five days.

John Butterfield won the contract, which was negotiated to provide an annual payment of $600,000 plus whatever revenue he could generate from express service and passenger traffic. As first laid out, the route began at Tipton, Missouri, a railhead 160 miles west of St. Louis. It passed through the cities of Springfield, Missouri; Fayetteville and Fort Smith, Arkansas; Sherman, Gainesville, Jacksboro, and Franklin (now El Paso) Texas; Tucson and Yuma, Arizona; and Los Angeles, California; a total distance of 2,795 miles.

The primary purpose of the Butterfield Overland stage line was to deliver the mail; construction of the first transcontinental railroad killed it.

The UT Institute of Texan Cultures at San Antonio, No. 73-1605

The only major change in the route was made in Texas in 1858, the same year service was begun. Obtaining water in West Texas posed a formidable obstacle, and the original route from Horsehead Crossing on the Pecos River followed that stream northwest to just south of the Texas-New Mexico border, paralleled that line west to the Guadalupe Mountains, swung into New Mexico for a short distance, looped back to Hueco Tanks east of Franklin, and then proceeded on to the Pass of the North.

In order to shorten the distance between waterholes, the route was changed to follow the same route being used by the San Antonio to San Diego mail route, a twice-monthly service begun in 1857. The new route ran from Horsehead Crossing to Fort Stockton, Fort Davis, Van Horn, Fort Quitman, and thence up the Rio Grande to El Paso. In 1858 the Butterfield line took over the mail route from El Paso to San Diego, although the service between San Antonio and El Paso continued until the outbreak of the Civil War in 1861.

For its time, establishing the Overland Mail was a tremendous undertaking. Butterfield spent nearly a million dollars in preparation. He bought about a hundred Concord coaches and hundreds of horses and mules. Nearly 150 way stations had to be located, established (and in many cases built), and staffed. Across much of North Texas, the projected route was through areas with no roads, and the aid of county commissioners in counties still-aborning had to be procured in getting primitive roads constructed. Fortunately for Butterfield, in other areas the route followed established military roads, although it must be remembered that these were no more than tracks defined by repeated use, not improved roads.

Butterfield well knew that he was entering upon an enterprise with a number of unknown factors. Appended to the company's first time schedule were several notes. "Remember that no allowance is made in the time for ferries, changing teams, &c. It is therefore necessary that each driver increase his speed over the average per hour enough to gain the necessary time for meals, changing teams, crossing ferries, &c. [Drivers were expected to average about 5 miles per hour.] Every person in the Company's employ will always bear in mind that each minute of time is of importance. If each driver on the route loses fifteen (15) minutes, it would make a total loss of time, on the entire route, of twenty-five hours, or, more than one day."

Butterfield also issued nineteen "Special Instructions" to his employees. Several are of particular interest.

1.–It is expected that all employees of the Company will be at their posts at all times, in order to guard and protect the property of the Company. Have teams harnessed in ample time, and ready to proceed without delay or confusion. Where the coaches are changed, have the teams hitched to them in time. Teams should be hitched together and led to or from the stable to the coach, so that no delay can occur by their running away. All employees will assist the Driver in watering and changing teams in all cases, to save time.

[From this it can be seen that working for "the Company" was a 24-hour-a-day, 7-days-a-week job. Not knowing exactly when a stage would arrive, workers had to be ready every minute to spring into action. As an example, the schedule called for west-bound coaches to leave Fort Chadbourne, Texas, on Tuesdays and Fridays at 3:15 P.M. East-bound coaches were to leave the same point at 1:15 A.M. on Wednesdays and Satur-days. With only a few hours separating the two times, a delayed or early arrival of one coach or the other could lead to conflicts, not to mention lost sleep if the westbound coach was late. See rule number 4 below.]

3.–Conductors should never lose sight of the mails for a moment, or leave them, except in charge of the driver or some other employee of the Company, who will guard them till his return. This rule must not be deviated from under *any circumstances*. They will also report to the Superintendent in all cases if Drivers abuse or mis-manage their teams, or in any way neglect or refuse to do their duty.

> It is expected that all employees of the Company will be at their posts at all times, in order to guard and protect the property of the Company.

4.–The time of all employees is expected to be at the disposal of the Company's Agents, in all cases, at stations where they may be laying over. Their time belongs exclusively to the Company; they will therefore be always ready for duty. [Obviously there were no wage and hour laws in effect then!]

11.–The rates of fare will, for the present, be as follows: between the Pacific Railroad terminus and San Francisco, and between Memphis and San Francisco, either way, $200. Local fares between Fort Smith and Fort Yuma not less than 10 cents per mile for the distance traveled....

12.–The meals and provisions for passengers are at their own expense, over and above the regular fare. The Company intend, as soon as possible, to have suitable meals at proper places prepared for passengers at a moderate cost.

13.–Each passenger will be allowed baggage not exceeding 40 lbs. in any case.

14.–Passengers stopping from one stage to another, can only do so at their own risk as to the Company being able to carry them on a following stage....

15.–All employees are expected to show proper respect to and treat passengers and the public with civility, as well as to use every exertion for the comfort and convenience of passengers.

18.–INDIANS. A good look-out should be kept for Indians. No intercourse should be had with them, but let them alone; by no means annoy or wrong them. At all times an efficient guard should be kept, and such guard should always be *ready* for any emergency.

Some of the above rules are especially interesting in light of the experiences of the only through passenger on the first westbound stage. Waterman L. Ormsby, a twenty-four-year-old reporter for the New York *Herald,* took on the task of riding the historic first stage and posting periodic reports of his passage. Some pertinent passages relating to the Texas portion of his trip are quoted and commented on below.

"As I told you in my last, we crossed the Red River at Colbert's ferry, eight miles below Preston, and found many improvements on the road in progress on the Texas side of the river, under the liberal management of Grayson County, in which the flourishing town of Sherman is situated, and where we arrived on Monday afternoon, September 20. [As noted earlier, parts of the road over which the Overland Mail coaches traveled were still being built even as service was inaugurated. Counties were willing to improve roads for the same reason towns would soon be vying for railroads to pass through them, the hope of economic benefits.] As we were now a day ahead of

time, we should not have found teams in readiness had not an express been sent in advance to notify Mr. Bates, the superintendent between Sherman and Fort Chadbourne. His part of the road was so poorly stocked with animals, and those he had were so worn out in forwarding stuff for the other parts of the line, that he had to hire an extra team of mules, at short notice, to forward the mail to the next station, and these were pretty well tired from working all day. Most of his stock consisted of wild mules which had just been broken, and the process had not fitted them very well for carrying the mail with rapidity. Our extra team, however, took us along pretty fast.

"...The first station after leaving Sherman was twenty miles distant, and our team travelled it in three hours, so that before we reached there the beautiful moonlight lit up the vast prairie, making its sameness appear like the boundless sea and its hills like the rolling waves.

"Here we stopped and had the first opportunity of witnessing the operation of harnessing a wild mule. First he had to be secured with a laretto around his neck, and drawn by main force to a tree or post; then the harness had to be put on piece by piece, care being taken to avoid his teeth and heels. Altogether, I should estimate the time consumed in the process at not less than half an hour to each wild mule, and that, when the mail has to wait for it, might, I think, much better be spent on the road. Indeed, I should quite as much deem it in accordance with the spirit of the age to see the mail wait for the leather of the mail bags or harness to be tanned. I was much amused by the process, but it seemed a little behind the age for the mail to wait for it, and no doubt when all the company's wild mules are tamed the mail will make better time.

"...Another disadvantage under which we labored, this trip, was that our road, for the most of the way, was nearly new, though Mr. Bates claims that from Sherman to Belknap at least forty miles are saved by it. It leads through the counties of Grayson, Cooke, Jacks, Montague, Wise, and Young, all of which contribute towards its expenses, and certainly it must be a favorite with some, for, though only opened one month before I passed over it, it was already pretty well marked with wagon tracks.

"...Just on the edge of the Lower Cross Timbers we came to a station on the new road, where we had the first of a series of rough meals, which lasted for most of the remaining journey. The house was built of rough logs laid together roughly, and the chinks filled in with mud. The house was about twenty feet square, forming one room, and was occupied by two men keeping bachelors' hall, as might well be judged from the condition of things, of which the reader may imagine.

"Our arrival was unexpected [due to the stage running ahead of schedule], and there was some bustle in getting both breakfast and the team ready. The breakfast was served on the bottom of a candle box, and such as sat down were perched on inverted pails or nature's chair [one's haunches]. There were no plates and but four tin cups for the coffee, which was served without milk or sugar. As there were six of us, including drivers and workmen, those not lucky enough to get a first cup had to wait for the second table. The edible—for there was but one—consisted of a kind of short cake, baked on the coals, each man breaking off his 'chunk' and plastering on butter with his pocket knife; ...Such...was our meal here, and we were advised by the host to 'hurry up before the chickens eat it'—which we did, to the no little discomfiture of the chickens. It tasted good to me, and I can assure you that it would doubtless taste as well to any one coming over the same route at the same rate of speed."

Speed may not be the correct term to describe the coach's rate of progress, but it will do for lack of a better one. Ormsby had left at 8:00 A.M. on September 16, and by the time he arrived at Sherman, four days, eight hours, and forty minutes had elapsed. The trip from Sherman on to Franklin [El Paso] took another two days, fourteen hours, and ten minutes. By the time he reached San Francisco, he had been on the coach for just short of twenty-four bone-jarring days. The average rate of travel for the whole trip was just under five miles per hour.

Ormsby realized he was not seeing the Overland Mail at its best on this maiden voyage. "The first trip had many difficulties which each succeeding trip will remove," he noted. "Every month new stations will be built, shortening the relays of horses, and the roads will be much improved. Even with the very short time which has been made, there were distances varying from thirty to one hundred and thirteen miles travelled without relays of horses...." The longest stretch

Indians sometimes attacked the stagecoaches. The more interesting detail in this photograph is the four mules pulling the coach. The mules were often half-wild and full of run, making the journey somewhat of a controlled stampede.

The UT Institute of Texan Cultures at San Antonio, No. 73-1414

was in Texas, between Horsehead Crossing on the Pecos River to Pope's Camp near the New Mexico border. That followed the second-longest stretch, seventy-five miles, between the head of the Concho River and Horsehead Crossing, and was followed by the third-longest stretch, from Pope's Camp to the Pine Station at the foot of the Guadalupe Mountains. Needless to say, the West Texas portion of the journey was perhaps the hardest on both animals and people.

The question naturally arises as to how passengers' physical comforts were provided for in the absence of any towns. Ormsby addressed the subject as follows. "...I have had many inquiries as to the means of procuring meals and sleeping, along the route, for individuals about to traverse it. Of course these are not to be procured as comfortably as in the Astor House or our own houses, and for much of the distance the traveller has to rough it in the roughest manner. From Red River to El Paso there are few accommodations for eating, beyond what are afforded by the company stations to their own employees. In time, arrangements will be made to supply good meals at these points. The first travellers will find it convenient to carry with them as much durable food as possible. As for sleeping, most of the wagons are arranged so that the backs of the seats let down and form a bed the length of the vehicle. When the stage is full, the passengers must take turns at sleeping. Perhaps the jolting will be found disagreeable at first, but a few nights without sleeping will obviate that difficulty, and soon the jolting will be as little of a disturbance as the rocking of a cradle to a sucking babe. For my part, I found no difficulty in sleeping over the roughest roads, and I have no doubt that any one else will learn quite as quickly. A bounce of the wagon, which makes one's head strike the top, bottom, or sides, will be equally disregarded, and 'nature's sweet restorer' found as welcome on the hard bottom of the wagon as in the downy beds of the St. Nicholas. White pants and kid gloves had better be discarded by most passengers."

A trip across America by the Butterfield Stage was not just a trip, it was an adventure of a lifetime. Remnants of some of the old stage stops still remain at places like the Pinery in Guadalupe Mountains National Park, Hueco Tanks State Park, and on private land along the route. Scars left by the rolling wheels remain in many places. Although the outbreak of the Civil War caused the line to cease operations on March 1, 1861, its history shows that the Butterfield Overland Mail was one of the most daring success stories in a growing America just learning its own strength.

⤎ 9 ⤏

Texas Gunfighters

GUNFIGHTERS, BY DEFINITION, SHOOT PEOPLE. Yet some did so with greater frequency than others. John Wesley Hardin claimed to have killed over forty people; Billy the Kid claimed twenty-one. While those numbers may have been subject to inflation, there is no doubt that a few gunfighters killed so many people that the death toll could not have been due simply to being in the wrong places at the wrong times. Something deeper and more sinister was at work. They killed people because they liked it.

My friend Mike Cox wrote an exhaustive study of the career of Henry Lee Lucas, a serial killer who claimed to have killed as many as two hundred people in the course of his career. In that book Mike noted a statistic that chilled me when I read it. The FBI compiled a psychological profile of serial killers, and based on that and the population of the United States, they estimated that at any one time there

are about thirty-five such individuals in the country.

It occurs to me that the worst of the gunfighters, those who killed and killed and killed, were themselves serial killers. They were Old West versions of Henry Lee Lucas.

Looking at gunfighters in that light, some similarities between them and Lucas emerge. All began their criminal activities early in life. A similarity I found particularly fascinating was travel. Lucas was always on the move. He drove like a man driven, committing murders all over the United States. Examining the careers of top gunfighters reveals that they, too, operated over a wide area. In fact, one of the most amazing things about them is that they showed up, gun spitting death, in so many different places. Another common characteristic is that they, like Lucas, killed suddenly and with little or no provocation or mercy. Duels in the middle of the street at high noon make good fiction, but they are exactly that. Real gunfighters did not often give their victims a fair chance. Killing is not about sport, it is about killing. That is where the pleasure came from, not from the thrill of proving oneself faster than the other fellow.

* * * * *

Scene from the *Police Gazette* shows Billy the Kid shooting a drifter who waved a pistol at him.

Texas Gunfighters

by Michael Stevens
Arr. Stevens/Seyer

Texas Gunfighters

by Michael Stevens

Wild Bill Longley, he'd kill for nothin'
Pull a trigger, and see a man fall

He'd shoot a black man like you'd sweep your floor
He said, "For Texas and the South, you all."

Death with a pistol, a big .44
But unashamed to kill with a shotgun, most agree

Vigilantes hung him once, this time he'd die
With no remorse, in front of thousands, come to see
A vicious killer pay his debt didn't he?

John Wesley Hardin, a preacher's son
Killed seven men before the age of seventeen

All the papers and dime novels
Claimed he was the fastest gun they'd ever seen

Tracked by a Ranger to Alabama
Was apprehended, in what almost was a comic duel

Then he went to prison for fifteen years
Studied law, read the Bible, taught Sunday school
Died by the gun on a barroom floor, a drunken fool

John King Fisher, a frontier dandy
Handsome youth, set out young on the trail of sin

Liked gold and silver, silk and linen
His chaparejos were made of Bengal tiger skin

This Mister Fisher, could charm the law
Ruled Maverick County and a gang with his deadly gun

He pulled some strings became a lawman
Was shot, in San Antonio, while havin' fun
A mother danced upon his grave when his life was done

Ole Ben Thompson, tried legal killin'
Rode with a company of Texas Rangers, wore the gray

One more young killer, started out in Austin
Killed blacks and soldiers, anyone got in his way

He was a gambler, owned a few saloons
A sick man, tormented by the things he'd done

Rode a train from San Antonio with John King Fisher
Raising hell, this drunken trip, was their last run
Two old gunfighters, plum full of holes, died by the gun

Of all the gunmen that roamed the west
Just four Texans on this list of infamy

Unless you choose to count ole Sam Bass
A robber hero, not too smart, and a Yankee

This famous image of the old gunfighters
A dark hero, makes good press, but it's mostly lies
The appetite of the reading public justifies
Not much has changed in a hundred years I realize

Not much has changed in a hundred years

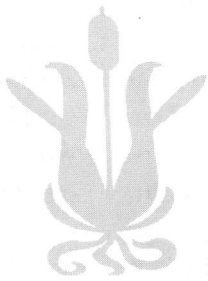

The parallel between serial killers of the Old West and those of today is supported by that friend of all writers, statistics. I love statistics for the same reason Mark Twain did. He said, "First, get your facts. Then you can distort them at your leisure." What he meant was that facts can be made to prove whatever you want them to, and this is exactly how I intend to proceed.

Another trick we writers use to beguile our innocent readers is to quote other writers (preferably well-known ones—see above). If something has made it into print, it must be right, right? If you believe that, just before I sell you that ocean-front property in Arizona, you might want to recall newspaper owner William Randolph Hearst's charge to his man in Cuba in 1898 when the Spanish-American War was furnishing no action: "You supply the pictures, I'll supply the war."

With that introduction, let's look at some interesting statistics furnished by Bill O'Neal in his book *Encyclopedia of Western Gunfighters*. (How's that for a neat trick? I get my statistics in a quote. They've just gotta be right.) O'Neal ranked thirty-three gunfighters based on the number of confirmable kills each had. Topping the list were Jim Miller, John Wesley Hardin, William Preston ("Wild Bill") Longley, Harvey Logan, Wild Bill Hickok, and John Selman. Just a little farther down the list were King Fisher, Billy the Kid, and Ben Thompson. (Save one,

all the subjects of this chapter appear on that list.)

Now I'll let you in on the ultimate writer's secret. When you really want to mess with people's minds, you take two unrelated facts and forge a connection between them, thereby making a point that is, to use a fitting phrase, bullet-proof. It can't be proved, but it can't be disproved, either. Observe.

When the FBI estimated that there were thirty-five people of the same twisted ilk as Henry Lee Lucas roaming the United States at any one time, the population of the country was (circa 1980) 220 million. During the peak gunfighter period in history, roughly 1870 to 1880, the population of the United States was about 40 million. Now, if serial killers existed in about the same proportion of the general population in both time periods, there should have been about six serial killers loose in the United States between 1870 and 1880.

Returning to O'Neal's list of gunfighters, we find that he credits Jim Miller with 12 killings, Hardin with 11, Longley with 11, Logan with 9, Hickok with 7, and Selman with 6. These top six on his list could very well have been serial killers. It would be hard to argue that these men were so dogged by bad luck that they just kept finding themselves in situations where they were forced to kill people. It is logical to believe they chose to kill because they were psychologically programmed to do so.

Close behind the top six were Fisher with 5, Billy the Kid with 4, and Thompson with 4. Were these men also serial killers? Or were none of them? It is possible that the numbers lie, but they do raise an intriguing possibility.

Another number does not lie: the number of lines of print devoted to reporting and, in many cases, glorifying the careers of these killers. The vast amount of copy written about them is proof positive of the fascination people have with such figures. The base appetites of a reading public fueled the transformation of many a murderer and thief into a Robin Hood of the range. (If you think such instincts are dead, peruse the headlines of the tabloids in the supermarket racks, or tune in to talk radio or television.)

Gunfighter songs point out the ultimate folly of their way of life. Those who lived by the gun died by it—or at the end of a hangman's rope.

Texas Gunfighters

Wild Bill Longley. Longley is perhaps unique among American gunfighters in that he was hanged twice—and some folks still believe he survived both times.

William Preston Longley is said by some to have killed as many as thirty-two people during the fifteen years of his gunfighting career. On one list of gunfighters, Longley ranked third in the number of victims of his gunplay. Born October 16, 1851, in Austin County, Texas, Longley came from what is usually called in such circumstances "a good family." His father, Campbell, was hardworking and had fought for Texas independence at the Battle of San Jacinto in 1836. It is hard to explain how a person from such a background could degenerate to the point that one writer said of him that "The only good thing that can be said of him is that he died young, and most of those who knew him thought that wasn't soon enough."

Longley entered his teenage years in the aftermath of the Civil War. Texas, like the rest of the South, was under military rule for a number of years. Former slaves were elevated to positions of authority, and white Southerners were not ready to accept the new order. Bill Longley made a lifetime habit of singling out blacks as objects of his hatred.

As a fourteen-year-old, Longley was an accomplished pistol shot reputed to be able to place six shots into an area the size of a plate while riding by at a gallop. At this same time he was seized of a desire for a pistol of his own, and he and a friend hopped a freight train to Houston, where he acquired a .44-caliber six-shooter. He and the friend also had a run-in with a black soldier, and Longley's friend killed the man with a knife.

Soon after, Longley killed a black soldier himself. The version told by the Longleys said the man rode by their ranch cursing all whites in general and Campbell Longley in particular. Bill ordered the soldier to surrender his gun, but the man fired at Longley. Bill's return fire struck the man in the head. He buried the body in a ditch. William Preston Longley was sixteen years old.

The measure of Wild Bill Longley can be taken from his next shooting scrape. He and a friend went to Lexington, in Lee County, Texas, to enter a horse in a race. Several blacks also entered horses in the race, and Longley and his friend decided they were not likely to collect even if they won. They withdrew and sulked until that evening. Then, as the blacks were swinging their partners in a street dance, the two youngsters charged on horseback, pistols blazing. Two people died and several more were wounded.

Inflated with his own self-importance, Longley was out of control. When a circus came to town, he demanded free admittance. Refused, he clubbed the owner into unconciousness and made the clowns dance a jig as he fired at their feet.

Longley had turned just plain mean, and he now went out of his way to kill people. Three black soldiers rode into the small community of Evergreen in Lee County where the Longley ranch was located. They stated they had heard people of their color were not welcome there, had some drinks at the bar, and left town. Someone got word to Longley, and he raced to town to uphold the "honor" of his race. Finding the men gone, he trailed them to their camp several miles away. As he rode up, one of the men fired a shot at him and received a bullet between the eyes in return. The others fled, and so did Longley. The law had finally taken notice of his activities, and he had to get out of the country.

You could take Wild Bill Longley from the scene of his killing, but you couldn't take the killing out of Longley. He left Lee County for Karnes County, where the Taylor-Sutton feud was raging. Approached one day by soldiers who mistook him for Charles Taylor, Longley fled, thinking they wanted him for the killing of the soldier near Evergreen. He outran all except the sergeant, and as the soldier pulled alongside demanding his surrender, Longley jammed his pistol into the man's side and killed him.

Now things were too hot for him in Karnes County. Longley returned home briefly, but his father sent him off to join a band of outlaws harassing Yankee soldiers in Bowie County, in the northeast corner of the state. Longley took up with Tom Johnson, a wanted horse thief, and one early predawn, vigilantes surrounded the house and dragged the two to a nearby tree for a necktie party. As the party raced away, they fired a number of shots at the two men kicking at the ends of the ropes. One bullet glanced off Longley's belt buckle; the other severed the rope. As his friend turned purple and gasped his last, Longley fell unconcious to the ground. In undoing their own work, the vigilantes sentenced to death the twenty-some-odd people Bill Longley was yet to kill.

After recovering, Longley joined the gang of outlaws and continued his killing ways. While riding with them he killed an estimated fifteen more men, including eight blacks, in a period of less than two years.

The traveling bug common to serial killers bit Longley hard about this time, and he headed north with a trail herd bound for Utah. Along the way Longley had one of the few bona fide quick-draw shootouts of his career. He and the trail boss quarreled, and the man challenged Longley to a shootout. Longley put six bullets into the man before he hit the ground.

Drifting now, Longley went first to Abilene and then to Leavenworth, Kansas. While drinking in a saloon in the latter town, Longley overheard a soldier making disparaging remarks about Texans. Longley whipped out his pistol and shot the man dead. He hid on a freight train headed for St. Louis, was captured and put in the military jail in Leavenworth, but bribed his way free. He headed for Wyoming, where after a few months he and an army quartermaster concocted a scheme to defraud the army in transactions involving livestock and supplies. Longley cheated his partner, was found out, and bushwhacked him. He got the death sentence, but this time he dodged hanging when the sentence was commuted. He escaped to the Indian Territory and hid out for a year, living with the Ute Indians.

Immediately upon his return to the white world, Longley killed again. In Parkersville, Kansas, in 1872, Longley argued over a card game and killed his opponent. His next actions showed just how devious and bold he had become, believing that the law could not touch him. When the dead man's father posted a $1,500 reward for his capture, Longley got two outlaw buddies to turn him in, collect the reward, and then break him out again. The trio split the money, and Longley hit the road for Texas.

Posses were soon looking for him, and he went to Comanche County to hide out with friends who lived there. While there he heard of a black man who had insulted a white woman and made it his business. He accosted the man, put two bullets into

> In undoing their own work, the vigilantes sentenced to death the twenty-some-odd people Bill Longley was yet to kill.

his head, and killed a member of the posse that took his trail.

Early 1875 found Longley working on a Bastrop County ranch where a brother was also employed. One day Longley got word that one of his cousins was dead. There were two versions of how the cousin had died. One said he had fallen off a horse and was killed. The other said that Wilson Anderson, one of Bill's boyhood friends, had killed him. Longley chose to believe the latter, and on April 1 he rode to Anderson's farm, found him plowing a field, and blew him away with a shotgun. Finally, Bill Longley had killed a man and would hang for it.

But three bloody years yet remained to Longley. Hiding out under an assumed name and working as a farmhand, he got into a quarrel with a local tough. Following a fistfight, Longley killed the man in a ride-by shooting that evening. Some months later Longley met another outlaw, Will Scrier, and the two decided to turn the other in for reward money. Longley struck first, but Scrier fought back with unbelievable fury: It took thirteen bullets to kill him.

Going to ground near Crockett, Longley found work as a woodcutter, using the name William Black. Two days before Valentine's Day, 1876, he stopped at a farmhouse and met Louvenia Jacks. He fell in love at first sight. Longley got a job working a nearby farm on shares for a local preacher, Roland Lay. Shortly he learned he had a rival for Louvenia's

affections: a cousin of Roland Lay. Lay took his kinsman's side and tried to discourage Longley's attentions; matters degenerated, and the partners parted company. Longley continued his courtship of Louvenia, however, and Lay swore out a warrant for his arrest, saying Longley had threatened his life—quite likely true. Longley was jailed, but he set fire to the jail and escaped.

Never one to pass up a chance at revenge, Longley borrowed a shotgun and went to Lay's farm. In Longley's own words, here is what happened. Notice the lack of emotion in the way he described killing Lay.

"I walked into the cowpen and stood between him and his gun. He looked up and saw me and turned white as a sheet. He seemed to know that his time had come and that he would get no mercy at my hands. When he saw me I told him it was the last of 'pea time' with him, and if he had anything to say he had better be at it. He said he hated to die and leave his wife and family. Then I asked him why he did not let me alone when I was at peace with him and all his kinfolk. To this he gave no answer and I dropped my gun to level with his body and fired. The gun was heavily loaded with turkey shot. He fell backwards and I left him."

Notice one other thing about Longley's remarks. He made no reference to the fact that he was a multiple murderer, was on the run and was in fact at that moment in hiding from the law, and as such had precious little to offer anyone, much less an innocent farm girl. He showed the total lack of remorse and shame that is the hallmark of the psychopath.

Wild Bill Longley did not know it, but he had killed his last man. On June 23, 1876, Governor Richard Coke offered a $500 reward for the murderer of Roland Lay. Longley fled to Louisiana and rented land from the local sheriff. He courted the man's daughter, and they became engaged. Then, perhaps feeling remorse for the first time in his life, he confessed his past life to her. She told her father, who armed himself and a deputy with shotguns and surprised Longley when he returned to the house from working in the field.

Returned to Giddings to await trial, Longley took to writing letters to Texas newspapers, once again giving some insight into his character. Editorial comments are inserted in brackets. "Well...I am condemned to die without the sympathy of a single human being that I can recall.... [He showed no sympathy for the dozens of people he gunned down.] I am willing to pay this debt for the good of the rising generation.... [He cannot admit that he is being punished for doing wrong, twisting even his own death into something good.] I have two dear brothers who are now in their boyhood, and are disposed to be wilder than I was, and I hope this will be a warning to them, for I would freely die, rather than see them live the life that I have been living, and yet I believe I have been the most successful outlaw that ever lived in Texas, as far back as I can remember." [What monumental gall! He attempts to ennoble himself once again and boasts of his success as though being the most prolific murderer of his time was an achievement to be proud of.]

Attempting to win sympathy for himself, Longley continued on in the same vein, lamenting his wasted life but never once commenting on the lives he had snuffed out or ruined, never expressing remorse for having killed but only regret for the fact that he had now to pay with his life for having done so. The closest he came to acknowledging responsiblity for his actions was at the end of the letter. "And now, boys, remember the road Bill Longley had travelled, in disobeying his parents, and when you start to do wrong remember that a very small wrong always leads to still greater ones, and so on until finally, nothing will seem wrong to you if you follow the wrong road. My first step was disobedience; next whisky drinking; next carrying pistols; next gambling, and then murder, and I suppose the next will be the gallows. I hope my father and mother will never be blamed for what I have done for they tried to raise me right."

Longley was convicted of the April 1, 1875 murder of Wilson Anderson and was sentenced to hang. October 11, 1878 dawned cloudy and threatening rain.

Some four thousand curious onlookers watched as the infamous murderer mounted the gallows completed only half an hour before the execution. With great bravado Longley inspected the gallows, commenting on the sturdiness of its construction and jumping up and down on the steps to test them. He made a brief speech in which he continued to show himself incapable of admitting any guilt of his own without simultaneously pointing a finger of guilt at others. "I hope you will all forgive me for anything I have done. I have already forgiven all that did anything to me. [He neglected to mention that he had also killed them.] I know I have to die, and I hate it, for we all hate to die when the time comes, for I have killed many men who hated to die as bad as I do...." [But none deserved to die as much as he did.]

Longley's arms and legs were bound, and a black hood was drawn over his head. Then the trap was sprung, and for a moment it seemed as though Wild Bill Longley had cheated the hangman for the second time. The rope slipped, and Longley plunged downward until his knees dragged the ground beneath the gallows. The sheriff and his deputies had to hoist Longley back into the air to finish the hanging.

Perhaps the bungled hanging explains what happened after Longley's death, perhaps not. At any rate, rumors began to circulate that the hanging was a sham. Some said the slipped rope kept his neck from breaking, and that he was taken down before he strangled. Others said the sheriff, with whom he had become friends, furnished him with a special harness that kept him from harm. According to these stories, Longley lived out the rest of his days in South America.

For decades the story that Longley had cheated death surfaced and resurfaced. A Louisiana man claimed that Longley was his grandfather. According to his story, Longley moved to Louisiana, took the name Captain John Calhoun Brown, and died in 1923 a respected member of the community with a large family.

Finally, in 1992, family members enlisted the assistance of Smithsonian Institution forensic anthropologist Douglas Owsley. Owsley compared photographs and handwriting samples of Longley and Brown and concluded that they could be one and the same. All agreed there was one way to find out: Open up Longley's grave and see if the bones therein, if any, were from a person matching Longley's description. If no bones were found, it would be an indication that Longley had in fact escaped the hangman's noose.

There was a catch, of course. No one knew where Longley's grave was. The original marker had long since disappeared, and searchers relied on old photographs and the memories of old-timers to pinpoint the most likely site. A backhoe was brought in, and nine graves were excavated. None were empty, and none contained the remains of a body that could have been Longley's. The search was called off, since it was obvious that no one had any idea where the grave actually was.

Did Longley escape, or is the story just another example of the Elvis syndrome? The answer depends on what you want to believe. Somewhere between 4,000 and 7,000 people witnessed the execution. One story says Longley's body was never seen by the public afterward. This story says the gallows was constructed so that the sheriff and a deputy were able to put Longley into a coffin out of view, and that he slipped out between the gallows and the grave. Another story says that three local doctors examined Longley and turned his head 180 degrees to show that his neck was broken.

Which story do you prefer? The answer may depend a great deal on whether you think you've seen Elvis lately.

John Wesley Hardin. Ranked second in the number of people he killed in gunfights was a preacher's son. Although that list records John Wesley Hardin as having killed 11 people to Jim Miller's 12, it accords another distinction to Hardin, that of having taken part in more gunfights—19—than any other man.

Leon Metz, an El Paso historian, put Hardin into perspective when he wrote, "John Wesley Hardin may well have been the West's greatest gunfighter, although this statement is a matter of opinion, judgment and interpretation. Certainly he was the most dangerous man ever to walk the wide and dusty streets of El Paso, and that community has known such manslayers as Dallas Stoudenmire, Pat Garrett, Wyatt Earp, John Selman, George Scarborough, Jeff Milton, Mannen Clements and Jim Miller."

Since Jim Miller was the only man ranked ahead of Hardin in the number of people slain in gunfights, and John Selman was the man who killed Hardin, Metz swung a pretty wide loop when he made that statement. I'm not about to try to prove him wrong.

Both Bill Longley and John Hardin grew up in post-Civil War East Texas and shared the dislike of their elders for Northerners and blacks, so perhaps it is not remarkable that their careers in crime share many common characteristics. Hardin was eighteen months Longley's junior, and both claimed a black man as their first victim, with many more to follow.

Hardin killed for the first time at the age of fifteen, although he nearly killed a playmate with a knife when only eleven. His first slaying was as senseless as many that followed. A former slave refused to

John Wesley Hardin committed his first murder at the age of 15, had slain 30 men by age 21, and lay dead on an El Paso barroom floor at 42,

Courtesy Leon C. Metz

step off a public road to let Hardin pass, and Hardin used three slugs from a .44 to gain the right-of-way.

This slaying led directly to three more within a short time. Hardin learned that soldiers were coming to arrest him for his first murder, and he set up an ambush at a creek. He blasted two from their horses with a shotgun and dispatched the third with his pistol. In another similarity with Longley's career, friendly ex-Confederates helped cover his getaway.

It was over a year before Hardin, now just over sixteen and with four murders against him, killed again. Hardin enjoyed the luck of the cards in a Christmas Day, 1869, game in Towash, a town on the Brazos River in Hill County, and one of the other players suggested that more than luck was involved. The two met later in the street. Hardin dodged a bullet and then fired two of his own. He did not miss.

Now on the run, Hardin displayed the same violent temper and disregard for danger that drew Bill Longley into so many scrapes. Even though he was hiding from the law, Hardin went to a circus in Horn Hill, in Limestone County. Hardin argued with a circus worker, who punched him and reached for a pistol. Again, John Wesley Hardin did not miss. Later that same month, January 1870, Hardin fell in with a young woman in Kosse who promised to show him a thing or two in a barn. Her boyfriend was waiting there with a gun and demanded Hardin's money. Hardin obliged, pitching the money to the floor. The eager bandit bent to pick it up, Hardin drew his pistol, and as the man looked up at the sound of a six-gun clearing leather, Hardin shot him between the eyes.

Not yet seventeen years old, John Wesley Hardin had already killed seven times, a number equal to Wild Bill Hickok's entire career. And Hardin had another twenty-five years to go.

Hardin headed for Louisiana, as Texas had become a trifle warm for him, but he was arrested in Marshall. He killed one of his guards and decided Mexico was the place to be. He was caught soon after heading south, but that same night a guard went to sleep on duty, and Hardin used his shotgun to make the man permanently drowsy.

Making his way to the home of relatives named Clements near Smiley, in South Texas, Hardin decided to join them on a cattle drive to Kansas instead of going to Mexico. Hardin killed two Indians in the Indian Territory before becoming involved in a full-scale gun battle. The boss of another herd pushed his animals too hard, and they overtook the Clements herd and became mixed with it. Separating them out was a hard job, and Hardin took the man at fault to task. One word led to another, and the two sides agreed to settle the dispute with guns. Hardin and his cousin Jim Clements went against six; when the smoke cleared,

Hardin had killed five and Clements the other.

Then it was on to Abilene, the end of the trail and the beginning of a big party for many drovers. Hardin celebrated by killing one man in a card game and another he caught prowling through his things one night. On his way back to Texas, he killed a Mexican who had killed a cowboy friend of Hardin's a few days earlier. He had been home only a couple of months when two black state policemen showed up in Smiley looking for him. Hardin confronted them in the general store as they ate lunch, killing one and wounding the other.

Hardin was now eighteen years old and had killed twenty men. He seems to have decided it was time to settle down, for he married Jane Bowen and started a family. If she had any hopes of a peaceful life of marital bliss, the notion was soon shattered. Hardin gambled at ten-pins and argued over the result. This time the outcome was not to his liking at all. Phil Sublet treated Hardin to a load of buckshot, and the law soon caught up with the wounded Hardin. He was jailed in Gonzales, but a friend slipped him a saw, and he was soon on his way to DeWitt County.

John Wesley Hardin showing up in DeWitt County was tantamount to throwing gasoline on a bonfire. The community was engaged in the bloody Sutton-Taylor feud, a battle between Southerners (the Taylors) and Union officials and their friends (the Suttons), who were supported by the local law. Hardin was related by marriage to the Taylors, and he took their part—in any case, he was against the law. Within the span of a few months Hardin gunned down first a deputy sheriff and then the sheriff. Again Hardin revealed a parallel between himself and the psychopathic Longley: After killing the sheriff, Hardin called him "a horror to all law-abiding citizens." Like Longley, Hardin considered himself to be righteous and everyone against him in the wrong.

Traveling, traveling, Hardin wound up in Comanche nine months later. There Hardin was celebrating his twenty-first birthday in a saloon when he was approached by Charlie Webb, a deputy sheriff. Both men drew, although it is not clear who acted first. Hardin took a bullet in the side as he put a slug into Webb's head.

Hardin was wearing out his welcome even in Texas. He ran for the East Coast; a mob caught his older brother Joe and a couple of others and lynched them. The state of Texas offered a $4,000 bounty for Hardin, and Louisiana put up money for his capture as well.

Four thousand dollars plus was a lot of money in 1874, and Texas Ranger John B. Armstrong, who, like most rangers,

> Hardin was now eighteen years old and had killed twenty men.

worked for very little money, set out to learn Hardin's whereabouts and capture him. A bit of detective work was required. Armstrong worked with a man named John Duncan, who rented a farm next to Hardin's father and kept his eyes and ears open. Learning that Hardin's father had a team and a wagon belonging to his son, Duncan asked to buy it. Hardin's father wrote his son asking permission to sell, and Duncan got a look at the envelope before it went off in the mail. It was addressed to John Adams, in Alabama. (Some accounts say Hardin was using the name J. H. Swain.)

That was enough for Armstrong. He asked that warrants be made out in both Hardin's real name and his alias and took out for Alabama. There he learned Hardin had just left for Florida for a short trip. Armstrong, Duncan, and some local officers waited for Hardin at a small station outside Pensacola. On August 23, 1877, the train pulled in with Hardin on board.

The plan was for the local officers to enter the rear of the car as Armstrong came in the front, facing Hardin, while Duncan would try to grab Hardin's right arm, which was resting on the window sill. The plan fell apart at the beginning. Armstrong drew his long-barreled Colt .45 frontier model, almost a trademark of the Texas Ranger, and burst in the door. Hardin saw the pistol and yelled, "Texas, by God!" as he reached for his own, which he had in the waistband of his trousers.

In a scene that would have been comical except for its potential deadliness, Hardin's pistol hung in his suspenders, and he almost pulled his pants off over his head trying to wrench it free. Meanwhile a compatriot of Hardin sent a bullet through Armstrong's hat and took one through the heart in return. By this time Armstrong had closed the gap, and he grabbed Hardin's pistol, wanting to take him alive. Hardin kicked like a cornered mule, sending Armstrong backward into the empty seat facing Hardin. Armstrong bounced back, swinging his heavy Colt at arm's length, and it crashed into Hardin's skull. When the outlaw awoke two hours later, he was on his way to jail in Texas.

But Armstrong was not out of the woods yet. In his rush to capture Hardin, he had left Texas without the warrants, arranging for them to be sent on by mail. The United States Post Office did its usual sterling job, and Armstrong was left holding a prisoner without a warrant in a state where he had no jurisdiction. Hardin's friends got him a lawyer and hauled Armstrong into court to show cause why he should be allowed to hold Hardin. Armstrong did some fancy talking and got the judge to agree to wait for the papers to arrive.

The reading of the warrant to Hardin provided another moment of high drama and demonstrated Armstrong's skill as a lawman. First Armstrong read the warrant naming Hardin. Hardin denied his identity, and in those days of no fingerprints, Armstrong lacking photographs, who was to say? Hardin then made a fatal mistake: He claimed he was John Adams. Armstrong whipped out the warrant naming John Adams and read it, ending with, "Now do you surrender?" Hardin owned up to his identity and cursed Armstrong all the way back to Texas for tricking him.

Kept in shackles and guarded by Texas Rangers around the clock, Hardin was tried for the killing of Charlie Webb in Comanche the last week of September, 1877. One of the rangers guarding him published an account of his experiences in the *Galveston News* and commented on the legend that Hardin was so tormented by memories of men he had killed that he could not sleep. "...I have guarded him at midnight, when the moonlight was reflected in the dew drops on the prairie sedge, and in the tangled brush that skirts the cow-house. Alone and standing among the sleeping rangers I have gazed on the face of him I guarded, John Wesley Hardin, the gentlest sleeper of them all. Sometimes a troubled look disturbed his countenance for an instant; once he murmured 'Johnny,' his little son's name, but in the main his sleep was calmer than the moonlit stream flowing past me to the sea. If any demons ever haunted his bedchamber, they kept aloof from his bivouac."

Hardin was found guilty and sentenced to twenty-five years at hard labor in the state penitentiary. He wept—not for his many crimes or victims, but for himself, saying the jury had been too hard on him.

While at Huntsville, Hardin studied law. He also read the Bible, taught Sunday school, and headed the debate team. He wrote extensively to his family, urging his children not to follow his example and telling of his plans, when released, to move his family to a small town and practice law. However, his wife died while he was in prison.

After serving fifteen years, Hardin was released, and shortly thereafter Governor Hogg pardoned him. His civil rights restored, he sought admittance to the bar and succeeded. Then he began seeking a place where a man of his background could fit in. He bounced from Gonzales to Junction and finally landed in El Paso. He is there still.

Hardin's dream of practicing law moldered while he hung out in saloons and gambled. Then he became involved with a local ex-prostitute, Helen Mroz (or Morose), and wound up arranging to have her husband murdered. One of the hired killers was John Selman.

The killers did their work, but Hardin did not enter into bliss with his girlfriend. Instead, for some reason, he went to pieces. Perhaps the realization that he was so far gone he had to hire others to fight his battles unraveled him. He drank heavily, gambled constantly, and quarreled with Mroz. Finally she left him, and

Hardin's days dissolved into one long drunk.

For some reason Hardin also quarreled with John Selman. Some say it was because Hardin did not share with Selman money taken from the dead Mroz. Regardless, as Hardin played at dice in the Acme Saloon one evening, Selman batted aside the swinging doors and rushed in, pistol roaring. Hardin fell dead, and for the next two hours townspeople trooped by for a look at the body lying dead on the barroom floor. John Wesley Hardin had finally gotten as good as he had given.

John King Fisher and Ben Thompson. Both Fisher and Thompson appear in Bill O'Neal's list of top gunfighters (*Encyclopedia of Western Gunfighters*), but they have more in common than that. I believe they are the only two gunfighters on that list to have died together in the same gunbattle. Both acted as lawmen at various times in their lives. Both were somewhat of a dandy, affecting a dudish style of dress. And it would be difficult to find two more cold-blooded and self-righteous killers. They were perfectly matched.

To recount fully the deeds and misdeeds of both Fisher and Thompson would take an entire book, so what follows is necessarily incomplete. As a measure of their stature, however, consider the name bracketed by theirs in O'Neal's list: Billy the Kid. Fisher ranks just above the Kid, Thompson just below. What Leon Metz noted about Fisher could apply to Thompson as well: "By all odds King Fisher should have become a better known figure than Billy the Kid or John Wesley Hardin. He had all the attributes: good looks, youth, style, color, deadliness and cold courage. Unfortunately he lacked a good press agent."

Fisher was born in 1854 in Collin County. His mother died while he was quite young, and he grew to hate his stepmother. Tiring of his being underfoot as she worked around the house, she would hang him by his suspenders from a nail driven over a doorway until she finished. His rebellious nature surfaced early, and at age sixteen he was sent to the state penitentiary for breaking and entering. At the time he was on the run, accused of horse stealing.

Following his release from prison, Fisher joined the bad element in the notorious Nueces Strip (see chapter 3). Swarms of murderers and thieves and a few honest people lived there. At the age of seventeen Fisher was already such an accomplished gunman that ranchers around Eagle Pass hired him to clean out the rustlers in the area.

John King Fisher was as handsome as he was deadly. Never brought to justice for the murders and other crimes he committed, he died of poor judgment in San Antonio, riddled by 13 bullets meant for companion Ben Thompson.

Courtesy Leon C. Metz

Fisher was quick to see the possibilities of living off other people's labors, and he started his own spread. He surrounded himself with the worst, most desperate men he could hire from both sides of the border, and soon the man who had run the other rustlers out was the biggest cow thief of them all. In addition, Fisher cowed what local law there was and set up what amounted to his own little kingdom, marking its boundary with a sign that read, "This is King Fisher's road. Take the other."

Fisher ruled his outlaws with the gun. Once four of his hands brought a herd of stolen cattle to the ranch, and they and Fisher went to work altering the brands. An argument arose over how much the men should be paid for the cattle, and both sides grew wary. In the midst of branding, one of the men bumped into Fisher. Fisher brained the man with the heavy branding iron he was holding, snatched his pistol from its holster, and shot the three men sitting on the fence before they could move.

Naturally, Fisher attracted the attention of Texas Rangers sent in to clean up the Nueces Strip. Ranger Captain Lee McNelly wrote to his superiors in Austin, "You can hardly realize the true conditions of this country. It is under a reign of terror from the men who infest this region. This county is unorganized and attached to Maverick county for judicial purposes. The white citizens are all friends of King Fisher. There is a regularly

organized band of desperadoes from Goliad to the headwaters of the Nueces. This band is made up of men who have committed crimes in other states and fled for refuge here, where they go to robbing for a living. They are organized into parties of twenty five to forty men each and form camps in counties, in touch with each other. They pass stolen horses along this line and sell them up north."

In the face of such organized resistance and with the local authorities either in King's pocket or afraid to act, even McNelly found it difficult to deal with Fisher. He took a party of rangers to Fisher's ranch and arrested him in June 1876. (Why he did not simply shoot him down as the rangers did many other desperadoes is a matter for conjecture, although the reason may have been that McNelly knew Fisher's wife was present.) Fisher, nine of his men, and eight hundred head of stolen cattle were taken to Eagle Pass, where local authorities turned all loose. King Fisher ruled supreme.

McNelly was furious. According to one of the rangers in his party, George Durham, Fisher was the first man McNelly had taken prisoner, and to see him promptly turned loose again was almost more than the ranger captain could bear. He knew the man was guilty, but he had no evidence that could be used in court. Dead outlaws never made bail; what could happen to a live one was something new to McNelly. The exchanges between the parties involved in Fisher's release show how out of place McNelly was when courts got involved. Durham related what happened.

"'My name's McNelly,' he said [to the deputy sheriff of Maverick County]. 'I'm a Ranger—Texas Ranger. I got nine prisoners I want to deliver.'

"'. . . very well, Captain. I see you've got Mr. Fisher.'

"'I've got King Fisher, yes.'

"'What charge, Captain?'

"'He's no stranger to you. He's a damn bandit and killer.'

"The lawyer spoke up. 'That's an opinion, Captain—not a charge under Texas law. You must name his bandit victims and produce them as witnesses. You must produce the bodies of his homicide victims, with proper witnesses.'

"McNelly was licked and said so, but he preached Fisher a little sermon before he turned him loose and warned him of the possible consequences of continuing his wicked ways. 'You could make a good citizen. You'd also make a nice corpse. All outlaws look good dead.'"

The next year, 1877, one of them was dead, but it was not the outlaw. McNelly died of tuberculosis, and Captain Lee Hall took out after King Fisher. This time proper charges were filed, and Fisher was jailed. To be sure friends did not arrange his release, he was kept in the county jail in San Antonio. Still, Fisher's charm over the law held. Despite twenty-one indictments and six jury trials, Fisher was never convicted of any of his Maverick County crimes.

In fact, Fisher had so much influence in Maverick County that he was appointed a deputy sheriff. While serving as such, he killed what was to be the last of his rumored twenty-some-odd victims. In the process of arresting two suspected stage robbers, the Hannehans, he shot Tom Hannehan dead. An interesting little tradition came out of this act that illustrates that not everyone was King Fisher's friend. After Fisher died, he was buried in Uvalde (where his body still lies, in the Pioneer Cemetery), and each year on the anniversary of her son Tom's death, Mrs. Hannehan piled brush atop Fisher's grave, set it on fire, and danced gleefully about.

An old adage has it that birds of a feather flock together, and that was certainly the case with King Fisher and Ben Thompson. The two were longtime friends; Thompson was said to have given Fisher a pair of chaps that set off his already showy stepping-out getup in spectacular fashion. One person described him thusly: "Fisher was the most perfect specimen of a frontier dandy and desperado that I ever met. He was tall, beautifully proportioned and exceedingly handsome. He wore the finest clothing procurable, the picturesque, border, dime-novel kind. His broad-brimmed white Mexican sombrero was profusely ornamented with gold and silver lace. His fine buckskin Mexican short jacket was heavily embroidered with gold. His shirt was of the finest and thinnest linen and open at the throat, with a silk handkerchief knotted loosely about the wide collar. A brilliant crimson sash wound about his waist, and his legs were hidden by a wonderful pair of chaparejos, or chaps as cowboys called them—leather breeches to protect the legs while riding through the brush."

The "wonderful chaparejos" that Thompson gave Fisher were made from the skin of a Bengal tiger. The story goes that Thompson saw the tiger in a circus, admired it, and tried to buy it. When the owner wouldn't sell, Thompson shot the tiger in its cage and then, apparently, convinced the stunned owner that a dead tiger was worthless, but the tiger's skin was worth something.

Thompson had a way of trying to get what he wanted regardless of legality. Although trained as a typesetter, he preferred gambling as a way of getting money. He liked fast living, and it eventually led to a death of the same kind.

Ben Thompson squared off in at least fourteen gunfights, more than Bill Longley, almost as many as Billy the Kid, and nearly double the number of Wild Bill Hickok. His first shooting was in Austin in 1858, when he was sixteen. He argued with a local black teenager, went home and got a shotgun, and returned to shoot the boy, although not fatally. Thompson got an early lesson in what happened to people who shot blacks: He got off by paying only court costs. Ben was paying attention, and the next year he pulled a similar stunt, shooting a member of a goose hunting party he argued with.

The victims of Thompson's next two shootings were on the wrong side of the law. In 1860 he helped rescue some children captured by Indians in Austin, killing at least one Indian in the fight. Later that same year, working in New Orleans, Thompson wounded a thief who broke into his place of employment.

Shooting people legally perhaps appealed to Thompson, as it did to many in those days, and he joined a company of Rip Ford's Texas Rangers during the Civil War. Gambling in Laredo with Mexican soldiers, Ranger Thompson won all the troops' money and their guns. When the soldiers' lieutenant demanded the guns be returned, Thompson refused, and as the officer drew his pistol, Thompson killed him and another soldier. After the war, Thompson continued killing soldiers, this time two or three American troops occupying Austin.

Like many Texans, Thompson followed Texas cattle to Kansas, but unlike most, he stayed and opened up a saloon. He and an old friend, Phil Coe, operated

> The "wonderful chaparejos" that Thompson gave Fisher were made from the skin of a Bengal tiger.

the Bull's Head Saloon in Abilene until Thompson, his wife, and child were hurt in a buggy accident. As the Thompsons were heading back to Texas, Wild Bill Hickok killed Phil Coe and closed down the saloon. Thompson later set up a gambling operation in Ellsworth, Kansas, with his brother Billy, and the two were involved in a three-way street shootout with local law officers and some other gamblers the Thompsons quarreled with. Thompson was charged with attempted murder, but when his accuser wisely failed to show up in court, the charge was dropped. Once again Ben Thompson had flouted the law and gotten away with not so much as a slap on the wrist.

Returning to Austin, Thompson opened a gambling house and soon got into a shooting scrape with two men who insulted his dandy-like appearance on the street, not knowing who he was. About this time Ben Thompson went totally out of control. He began shooting up his own and other gambling parlors over wrongs real and imagined. He wandered about the streets of Austin shooting out streetlights and generally raising hell.

In 1879 Thompson surprised everyone by running for Austin city marshal. He lost, but in 1881 he ran again and won. In the meantime he had hired one of his lawyers to write his biography. Apparently by this time Thompson was mentally unbalanced. Or perhaps he really believed that he was one of Austin's finest citizens—certainly no one was willing to risk getting shot by telling him otherwise.

Ironically, despite the fact that almost everyone in Austin was his enemy, Thompson had to go to San Antonio to become embroiled in the row that was finally to do him in. Thompson had, for unknown reasons, had a falling-out with Jack Harris, a former friend who owned the Vaudeville Theater in San Antonio. Thompson took his two children to San Antonio to visit friends, and while they were thus occupied, he stopped in at Harris' place for a little sport at cards. Shortly he accused the dealer, Joe Foster, of cheating and backed out of the place with his pistol in his hand.

Word reached Thompson that Harris no longer wished to see his countenance and had, in fact, vowed to bring a double-barrelled shotgun into play should Thompson show his face at the Vaudeville again. Naturally, Thompson could not leave well enough alone, so on a later trip to San Antonio he swaggered into the Vaudeville, ordered a drink, and demanded to know the whereabouts of the man with a shotgun looking for him. Everyone claimed ignorance, and Thompson left, but unable to resist pushing his luck, he returned later to get something to eat. This time Harris was present, and hearing of Thompson's approach, he armed himself with his shotgun and stood against the wall where he could watch the swinging doors into the street.

Thompson didn't bother to come through the door. He fired through it, two shots hitting Harris, who died later that night. Thompson walked over to the Menger Hotel next to the Alamo and checked into a room. Next day he surrendered to the sheriff and resigned as Austin city marshal. Six months later a jury found him not guilty of Harris' murder.

If Thompson had had any sense at all, he would have quit while he was ahead. But he was a gambler, and he just couldn't stop himself. He drank even more heavily, caused numerous rows in Austin, and fired off his pistol whenever and wherever he felt like it. Now unable to sleep most nights, he roamed the city, and trouble was his constant companion. Perhaps he was fighting off a deep depression with his constant antics, but eventually even terrifying Austin was not enough to keep him amused. He had to go back to San Antonio.

And who should show up in Austin but an old friend, John King Fisher. Fisher was now in his "respectable" period as deputy sheriff of Maverick County and was the unopposed candidate for sheriff in the upcoming election. He was in Austin on official business and was about to return home. Thompson decided to accompany him as far as San Antonio, where he could take in a play and perhaps twist some less familiar tails for a change.

Fisher and Thompson began drinking before leaving Austin and continued on the train. By the time they reached San Antonio they were not in condition to display their best judgment. After they attended the play, nothing would do but that Thompson pay another visit to the Vaudeville Theater.

The visit was short, and it was his last.

Generous man that he was, Thompson walked into the Vaudeville and announced to the bartender that all the troubles of the past were forgotten and forgiven. He asked to see the owners, one of whom was now Joe Foster, the man he had accused of cheating him at cards, thereby bringing on the fatal confrontation with Harris.

Foster and several employees joined Fisher and Thompson in an upstairs booth for a drink. The drunken Thompson insisted on making a show of patching things up with Foster and grabbed for his hand to shake it. Foster was not about to shake the hand of the man who had called him a cheat and killed his friend Harris, and he backed away. Thompson slapped Foster and pulled his pistol, sticking the barrel into his mouth. One of Foster's men grabbed Thompson's gun, and suddenly thundering guns filled the air with flying lead.

Exactly what happened was never learned, because all the survivors had as their first interest avoiding being charged with murder. The only things known for certain are that Foster was shot in the leg and later died, while Fisher and Thompson died on the spot. And well they might. Fisher was shot thirteen times; Thompson nine, five in the head. The suddenness of their execution may be inferred from the fact that Fisher never drew his weapon, and Thompson got off but one shot, that probably the result of his pistol being grabbed.

Thompson and Fisher are perhaps the best examples of gunfighters who had the opportunity to go straight but just could not seem to avoid trouble. It did not have to find them; they sought it out, and in the end that was their undoing.

Sam Bass. It says something about Texas in the 1870s that Sam Bass, a prolific stage, train, and bank robber, was the first Yankee to become popular in the state following the Civil War. It says something about Texas today that people still gather in Round Rock each year to watch a reenactment of the shootout in which Bass received his fatal wound. He is perhaps as popular today as then.

Much of Sam Bass' popularity can be explained by the time in which he lived. Reconstruction times were hard in Texas, and what money was made seemed all too often to be sucked up by banks, railroads, the "gummint," and big businesses from back East. A lot of people liked Sam Bass because he twisted a few of those tails.

However, not all of Sam's public appeal can be so explained. Wild Bill Longley and John Wesley Hardin were his contemporaries and did more to offend the hated Yankees and Carpetbaggers running the state than Bass ever dreamed of. Perhaps it is indicative of a residue of respect for the law that Bass, a robber,

was more popular than the killers. In a way he was more respectable, sort of a white-collar criminal of the day.

Bass was the subject of a popular ballad that gave a fairly accurate outline of his career. It ends with the episode that the citizens of Round Rock still celebrate:

Sam rode into Round Rock
On July the twenty-first.
They riddled him with rifle balls
And emptied out his purse.
Sam is now a corpse
And six feet under clay.
And Jackson's in the bushes
Trying to get away.

In the end, Sam Bass was no luckier than the rest. Of 255 gunfighters listed in O'Neal's *Encyclopedia of Western Gunfighters,* 57 percent died of gunshot wounds. Their average age when they died was thirty-five. Sam Bass didn't make it that long. He died on his twenty-seventh birthday.

Sam Bass was born near Mitchell, Indiana, on July 21, 1851. He left home at age eighteen, heading south, and by the time he arrived in Texas in 1870, he had acquired considerable skill with playing cards and pistols. In this respect he fitted in rather well in his new home.

After working as a farmhand and teamster for several years, Bass scraped together enough money to invest. He invested it in a fast-stepping little pony that, while not the fastest racehorse in Texas, was quick enough to show Sam there were easier ways to make money than chopping cotton and chousing

Sam Bass liked to gamble and he liked the ladies, and the easiest way to get the money for both was to take what belonged to other people.

From Texas: 1874

mules. After Sam's "Denton mare" began winning races in 1875, he never did an honest day's work again.

Sam began to deal in horses and cattle—other people's, mostly. Driving cattle to Kansas was popular, so Sam and companions put together a herd, too, although they had to sneak it through Kansas and Nebraska to the Black Hills of South Dakota, where a gold rush centered around Deadwood. Money flowed freely there, and hungry miners were not too knowledgeable or particular about the proper brands being on cattle they bought.

For a time Sam and his partner went into the freight business, but winter snows closed the roads, and Deadwood's gambling houses and soiled doves offered a number of ways to warm the body and the blood. However, the pair soon fell victim to gold fever and bought a mine they were convinced would make them rich. Instead, it made them poor—flat broke, in fact.

Honest labor seemed to be getting them nowhere fast, so Bass and his friend acquired some new friends and a new occupation: stagecoach robbing. Seven stages serving Deadwood fell victim in short order, but the highwaymen seemed still to be on the road to nowhere. They bungled their first holdup, killing the driver but failing to get any money, and later attempts netted them only slightly greater hauls—in one case $11, in another a dozen peaches.

Thinking bigger must be better, the Bass gang decided to try robbing trains instead. For once Bass was right. In September 1877 they boarded a Union Pacific train when it stopped to take on water at Big Spring, Nebraska. Bass and his gang first worked the passengers, taking according to one account $13,000 and four gold watches. In the baggage car, they were informed the safe could not be opened. Disappointed, someone opened one of several nondescript wooden boxes. Glinting in the lantern light were hundreds—thousands—of bright, shiny, freshly minted $20 gold pieces. The boys were rich.

The gang split the money and parted company, traveling in three pairs. Three of the men were soon captured, one was never heard from again. Bass and his companion bought a buggy, threw their booty in and piled gear on top, and headed for Texas. Within a short time Bass showed up—alone—in Denton County. He spent freely and soon felt the need to replenish his coffers. Figuring what had worked in Deadwood would work in Denton, he got a gang together and began robbing stagecoaches. It did not take long to learn that stagecoaches in Texas carried no more money than ones in the Dakota Territory.

Let's see, Sam Bass asked himself, What can one do when robbing stagecoaches doesn't work? I know! We'll rob trains!

Sam Bass may have been a popular and likable fellow, but he was not blessed in the brains department. In the span of fifty days in early 1878, Bass and his gang robbed four trains within twenty miles of Dallas. Either Bass was an incredible optimist or was unbelieveably stupid not to realize that such a flurry of stage and train robberies would attract more law than any gang of road agents could handle. To make matters worse, after every robbery, a clear trail headed straight for Denton County.

Everybody knew who was responsible, and newspapers swarmed over the story, dubbing the gang Sam Bass and Company. A lot of small, poor farmers enjoyed the thought of somebody sticking it to the banks and railroads and getting away with it.

Sam no doubt enjoyed all the media attention, but another development any right-thinking idiot could have predicted became his undoing. Rewards were posted, and every bounty hunter, railroad agent, and Pinkerton detective with any ambition at all flocked to Dallas to try to capture Bass. One estimate had at least 150 men combing the bushes of Denton County for Bass and Company. In addition, a special company of Texas Rangers was organized, headed by June Peak.

You might say everybody in North Texas wanted to go Bass fishing.

Little more than three months after the Texas Rangers got into the act, the party ended. The rangers began by arresting anyone who helped the gang in any way, including lawyers. The heat forced the gang to move, and on May 12 Peak's rangers and sheriff's officers found Bass and Company in Wise County, killed one, and captured all their horses.

Bass sightings sprouted all over North Texas like the spring grass. The gang was reported to be in numerous localities buying horses, guns, and supplies, but confirmed sightings were not to be had. At the same time, the Texas Rangers virtually stopped their patrols. Speculation ran wild. Why had the rangers given up the chase?

The reason was the rangers knew something no one else did. One of the men arrested during the roundup of Bass accomplices was Jim Murphy, who proposed a secret deal with the rangers. He would attach himself to the gang and feed information on their whereabouts and activities to the lawmen.

Now that the rangers had an inside man, it was only a matter of time before Bass was caught. As the gang moved about, Murphy managed to post a series of letters detailing their plans, although not without arousing their suspicion. When Bass took them south to rob the bank at Round Rock, Murphy busily scribbled and mailed notes to the law from Belton and then Georgetown.

On the trip south the party stopped in at the Ranch Saloon in Waco for a beer, and there Sam Bass laid down the last $20 gold piece from the Nebraska train robbery. He wasn't worried, he told Murphy. "I will get some more in a few days. So let it gush! It all goes in a life-time." Sam Bass probably never came closer to stating his philosophy of life, one that got him killed at an early age.

When one lives from hand to mouth, there is mighty little room for error.

When the gang's plans to rob the bank at Round Rock became known, Texas Rangers rushed to get there before them. Even while Bass and his crew were

Bass spent his last $20 on a good time in Waco, then headed for Round Rock to make a withdrawal from the bank. Texas Rangers closed his account permanently.

From Texas: 1874

camped near the cemetery outside of town, going into town twice to scope out the situation, rangers were filtering in undercover. By the time the gang made its way into town on Saturday, July 20 (not the 21st as stated in the song quoted earlier), the place was crawling with rangers posing as bench-sitters.

Then one of those things happened that no matter how you try to explain it, it always comes out that somebody took his brain out of gear before he popped the clutch on his mouth. Bass and two others stopped at a store next to the bank to buy some tobacco before making their withdrawal. Deputy Sheriff A. W. Grimes noticed the men as they were walking down the street and decided that one of them had a gun hidden under his clothes. He followed them into the store, put his hand on the man's side (some accounts say it was Bass), and asked, "Say, Mister, are you carrying a gun?"

Now, Grimes knew the Bass gang was in town, knew they were there to rob the bank, and knew this trio looked suspicious. You tell me why he acted as he did.

At any rate, Grimes did not have long to ponder his mistake. One of the gang smoked him on the spot, and again accounts differ as to whether or not Sam Bass killed his first and only man there. The three broke from the store at a dead run. In another unexplainable bit of stupidity, they had tied their horses in an alley off a side street. Lumbering down the street in their high-heeled cowboy boots, the outlaws dodged a rain of gunfire from rangers and townspeople. One bandit fell dead, shot in the head, and Bass took a bullet low in the back. His remaining confederate helped Bass onto his horse, and the two galloped away.

Sam Bass spent the night before his twenty-seventh and final birthday moaning under a tree north of town. A posse found him there early the next morning and took him to town, where a doctor tended his wounds. The Texas Rangers encouraged the dying man to name his companions, but he refused. "It's against my profession. If a man knows anything he ought to die with it in him." Told he would not live out the day, he said, "Let me go." Then, minutes later, "The world is bobbing around!" And he was dead.

One member of the gang escaped— Frank Jackson, the man who helped Bass on his horse and out of town. What happened to him is unknown, but evidence is growing that he lived out his life in New Mexico and has surviving relatives there. Jim Murphy, the man who led the rangers to Bass, died by his own hand less than a year after the botched robbery attempt. He so feared retribution from Jackson or some other gang member that he chose to poison himself rather than risk being murdered.

I once taught school with a junior high English teacher who loved to quote fractured poetry. One of my favorites was, "Oh what a tangled web we weave/When first we practice to deceive./But when we've practiced for a while/How vastly we improve our style."

Poor Sam Bass practiced and practiced, but he just never got the hang of being a badman. Maybe that means he wasn't really bad at all. His tombstone asks a question Bass may have asked himself as he lay bleeding on the prairie all that lonely night before he died: "Why was he not true?"

Bibliography

Abernethy, Francis E. *Singin' Texas*. Dallas: E-Heart Press, 1983.

Adams, Ramon F. *The Old-Time Cowhand*. New York: Macmillan, 1961.

Breihan, Carl W. *Great Gunfighters of the West*. San Antonio: The Naylor Co., 1971.

Cox, Mike. *The Confessions of Henry Lee Lucas*. New York: Simon and Schuster, 1991.

_____. *The Texas Rangers*. Austin: Eakin Press, 1991.

Dixon, Olive K. *Life of "Billy" Dixon*. Austin: State House Press, 1987.

Dobie, J. Frank. *Cow People*. Boston: Little, Brown and Co., 1964.

_____. *The Longhorns*. Boston: Little, Brown and Co., 1941

Durham, George, and Clyde Wantland. *Taming the Nueces Strip*. Austin: University of Texas Press, 1962.

Gard, Wayne. *The Chisholm Trail*. Norman: University of Oklahoma Press, 1954.

Greer, James K. *Texas Ranger: Jack Hays in the Frontier Southwest*. College Station: Texas A&M University Press, 1993.

Hacker, Margaret Schmidt. *Cynthia Ann Parker: The Life and the Legend*. El Paso: Texas Western Press, 1990.

Haley, J. Evetts. *Charles Goodnight, Cowman and Plainsman*. Norman: Univ. of Oklahoma Press, 1936, 1949.

Hunter, J. Marvin. *The Trail Drivers of Texas*. Nashville: Cokesbury Press, 1925.

Lea, Tom. *The King Ranch*. Boston: Little, Brown, and Co., 1957.

McLuhan, T. C. *Touch the Earth: A Self-Portrait of Indian Existence*. New York: Promontory Press, 1971.

Metz, Leon C. *The Shooters*. El Paso: Mangan Books, 1976.

Newcomb, W. W. Jr. *The Indians of Texas*. University of Texas Press, Austin, 1961.

O'Neal, Bill. *Encyclopedia of Western Gunfighters*. Norman: Univ. of Oklahoma Press, 1979.

Ormsby, Waterman L. *The Butterfield Overland Mail*. San Marino: The Huntington Library, 1942.

Rathjen, Frederick W. *The Texas Panhandle Frontier*. Austin: University of Texas Press, 1973.

Robinson, Charles. *The Frontier World of Fort Griffin*. Spokane: Arthur H. Clark Company, 1992.

Simons, Helen, and Cathryn A. Hoyt. *Hispanic Texas: A Historical Guide*. Austin: University of Texas Press, 1992.

Wallace, Ernest, and David M. Vigness. *Documents of Texas History*. Austin: The Steck Company, 1963.

Webb, Walter P. *The Texas Rangers: A Century of Frontier Defense*. 2nd ed. Austin, University of Texas Press, 1965.

Wilbarger, J. W. *Indian Depredations in Texas*. Austin: Hutchings Printing House, 1889; facsimile edition 1985, Eakin Press, Austin.

Wilkinson, J. B. *Laredo and the Rio Grande Frontier*. Austin: Jenkins Publishing Co., 1975.

Index

About the Author

Larry D. Hodge is a full-time freelance writer from Marble Falls, Texas. Born in Elgin, Texas, Hodge attended the University of Texas at Austin. He taught junior high Texas and American history before joining a textbook publishing company as an editor, where he edited and wrote elementary, secondary, and adult education textbooks in many subject areas.

Since becoming a full-time writer in 1984, Hodge has become one of the best-known Texas writers in the fields of travel and the outdoors. He is a frequent contributor to *Texas Highways* magazine and is executive editor of Texas Parks and Wildlife Press. He also continues writing for the educational market and is the author of an economics textbook, a four-book reading series, and a pre-GED computer software program, all published by Steck-Vaughn Co. of Austin. Excerpts from his work are featured in a literature series published by Glencoe/McGraw Hill.

Hodge is also the author of several travel guidebooks, including *The Texas Dog Lover's Companion*, published in 1998 by Foghorn Press; *Backroads of Texas*, Fourth Ed., published in 2000 by Gulf Publishing, Co.; *Good Times in Texas*, published in 1999 by Republic of Texas Press; and *The Official Guide to Texas Wildlife Management Areas*, published in 2000 by Texas Parks and Wildlife Press.

Hodge's travel and outdoor writing grew from a love of Texas. He feels extremely fortunate to be able to make a living doing what he loves best—writing about the greatest place in the world to live.

A few thoughts from Michael Stevens about the music....

The Chisholm Trail
It has been said that there is a verse for every mile of the trail. We left out a few.

Bury Me Not on the Lone Prairie
Now I wonder why I never learned this before. I hated to edit it....there were so many good verses.

Streets of Larado
Usually I do this a cappella, but on tape it seemed a bit long so Larry suggested the guitar.

Fort Griffin and the Flat
This place sounded so awful I was worried about coming up with something, however it's now one of my favorite pieces.

Cynthia Ann "Preloch"
My favorite part is the Comanche phrase at the end, which means "those who have gone on," their way of saying Land of the Dead. I hope I didn't butcher their language too badly. For this phrase and my brief introduction to Comanche religion, I wish to thank Reaves Nahwooks of Cache, Oklahoma. This is a "Song of Spirit" with so little real facts. I hope it is acceptable to her descendants.

Gunfighters
I hope Larry is not upset that I paid little mind to Sam Bass. (L.H. says he is pleased...he never liked him anyway.)

Butterfield Stage
I had in mind this sounding like old movie and TV themes. Sort of Roy Rogers meets Frankie Lane kind of thing.

Two Texas Steers (Old Blue and Sancho)
My old "Lounge Lizardness" was showing. My wife, Alice, likes it best.

Adobe Walls
The last piece I wrote. This was a fast project for me, and I was running out of time, writing on the plane and in hotel rooms, pulling over on the road on the way to Austin to record the CD. It is the most powerful piece to me.

About the Musicians

Michael Stevens, Voice, Guitar, Composer

Cowhand, cowboy poet, custom guitar maker, singer, and songwriter Michael Stevens brings a lifetime of western and musical experiences to *Texas Tales in Words and Music.* He was born in 1945, on a farm in Newcomerstown, Ohio, where he grew up and trained with quarter horses. Like many Texans of today he got here as fast as he could, choosing to attend Texas Christian University in Fort Worth because they had a rodeo club.

After college, Stevens lived for a time in California where his work with repairing and building guitars began with Larry Jameson's Guitar Resurrection. In the late seventies he moved to Austin, opening his own shop, Stevens Guitars, Inc., where he built guitars such as the Christopher Cross doubleneck, the Roscoe Beck/Spencer Starnes/Roy Vought six string basses, and the Junior Brown Guit-Steel, a combined Telecaster-lap steel guitar. He became part of the blossoming Austin music scene and recorded with the Austin Lounge Lizards; he has appeared with such musical greats as Don Edwards, Asleep at the Wheel, and Junior Brown. Some of his fondest memories are of live performances at Big Bend legend Hallie Stillwell's birthday parties; he also sang at her wake.

Stevens' skill as a luthier led to his being asked, in 1986, to found the custom guitar shop for Fender Musical Instruments. During this return to California, he created a line of instruments for Fender that also bears the Stevens name. He built all the signature guitar prototypes for top players of the day; one built for Eric Clapton fetched $107,000 at a Christie's auction.

In 1991 he founded Stevens Electrical Instruments in Alpine, Texas, and continued to build guitars for the stars; notes from Stevens guitars accompany George Strait and Clint Black, among many others.

Alpine's Old West setting proved ideal for Stevens, allowing him to work as a cowhand on area ranches and also perform western songs and cowboy poetry on the very soil from whence sprang the genre.

When Larry Hodge went looking for someone to ride the trail with him on this project, he knew exactly where to find the best person for the job. Stevens approached the task of writing the songs in true western fashion. "I decided to take each chapter as law and use those facts and nothing but." He says, "Cowboys would call it 'riding for the brand.'"

Stevens brought something else to the project as well: a wealth of contacts in the musical world that added immeasurably to the quality of this recording. From backup musicians to Larry Seyer at Electric Larryland in Austin, Michael assembled a talented team that used New West technology to produce an album of Old West songs. The results border on magical.

Tom Middleton, Resophonic Guitar

Tom is an Austin resident, and has been playing the resophonic guitar since 1973. He is a frequent participant in cowboy poetry and music gatherings throughout the West, and has accompanied a wide range of popular western performers.

Richard Bowden, Violin, Mandolin

Richard's father was a professional country singer/songwriter, and so he grew up in a house of music. When he was just seventeen Richard began to search for a way to make his own music. He tried his mom's violin, and immediately began to spend hours in his room playing along with every record in his collection. He has been playing ever since and has appeared on hundreds of albums and on stages all over the world. He has worked with artists such as Terry Allen, Butch Hancock, The Maines Brothers Band, Joe Ely, and the Austin Lounge Lizards.

David Polacheck, Banjo

David Polacheck was born in 1947 to parents then resident in Greenwich Village in Manhattan. At an early age he became exposed to traditional folk music as his father, Charles Polacheck, had been both an aficionado and a performer of American folk music. When he was fifteen, he was inspired by a friend to consider learning to play the five-string banjo and has been dedicated to exploring the potential of the instrument ever since. His main influences in banjo playing have been Pete Seeger, Wade Ward, Hobart Smith, Dock Boggs, and Uncle Dave Macon. David has played with many bands over the years including The Possum Hunters, Brown's Mule, The Travis County Boys, The Four Cent Cotton Pickers, The Polacheck Brothers and Maggie, and his current group, The Blue Buckskin Whinchers. David resides in Austin, Texas, with his wife, Karen, who is also a member of the band.

Paul Glasse, Mandolin

An acoustic and electric mandolinist based in Austin, Texas, throughout an eclectic career as a bandleader and free-lance sideman Paul Glasse has played with a diverse assortment of musicians. Below is a partial list. Paul worked with some of these musicians for years. Other names reflect a one-time performance or recording session. Either way, at one time or another, Paul Glasse has recorded or performed on stage with:

photo by Nine François

Christine Albert, David Amram, Al Anderson, Darol Anger, Asleep At The Wheel, Mike Auldridge, Austin Lounge Lizards, Marcia Ball, Junior Brown, Arthur Brown, Jackson Browne, Cliff Bruner, Jethro Burns, Johnny Bush, Ray Campi, Mary Chapin Carpenter, Shawn Colvin, Smokey Dacus, Jimmy Day, Hazel Dickens, Floyd Domino, Jerry Douglas, Betty Elders, Gene Elders, Joe Ely, Steven Fromholtz, Jimmie Dale Gilmore, Johnny Gimble, Matt Glaser, David Grisman, David Halley, Slide Hampton, Butch Hancock, Roy Head, Bugs Henderson, Tish Hinojosa, Flaco Jimenez, Santiago Jimenez Jr., Steve Jordan, Kerrville All-Stars, Hal Michael Ketchum, Lee Konitz, Alison Krauss, Howard Levy, Laurie Lewis, Lyle Lovett, Mike Marshall, Katy Moffatt, Abra Moore, Tom Morrell, Willie Nelson, Gary P. Nunn, Tim O'Brien, Chris O'Connell, Marc O'Connor, Shawn Phillips, Maryanne Price, Gene Ramey, Leon Rausch, Francine Reed, Herb Remington, Riders In The Sky, Jim Rooney, Peter Rowan, Tom Rush, Shake Russell, Patty Scialfa, Eldon Shamblin, Michelle Shocked, Texas Shorty, Darden Smith, Red Steagall, Brad Terry, Floyd Tillman, Tony Trishka, UT Jazz Orchestra, Don Walser, Mitch Watkins, Claude Williams, and Peter Yarrow.

Michael Stevens
Texas Tales in Words and Music

Exec Producer: Republic of Texas Press
Producers: Mike Stevens and Larry Seyer
Guitars: Mike Stevens, Larry Seyer
Mandolin: Paul Glasse, Richard Bowden
Fiddle: Richard Bowden
Dobro: Tom Middleton
Banjo: David Polacheck, Paul Glasse
Bass: Spencer Starnes
Drums: Larry Seyer

photo by Nine François

photo by Nine François

photo by Nine François

Warning: Opening the CD package makes this book non-returnable.